The Art of Strategic Innovation

Alex on Finance, Volume 2

Alex Thompson

Published by Side Hustle Success, 2023.

THE ART OF STRATEGIC INNOVATION

First edition. July 5, 2023.

ISBN: 979-8215314296

Written by Alex Thompson.

Also by Alex Thompson

Alex on Finance
Financial Freedom Roadmap - Achieving Early Retirement through the FIRE Movement
The Art of Strategic Innovation

Standalone
Side Hustle Success: Unlocking Your Entrepreneurial Potential
Side Hustle Success: The Ultimate Guide to Passive and Financial Freedom
Mastering the Markets: Advanced Trading Strategies for Success and Ethical Trading Practices
Financial Fortitude

Table of Contents

Chapter 1: Introduction

1.1 Definition of Cryptocurrencies

Cryptocurrencies have emerged as a disruptive force in the realm of finance and investment. In order to understand the pros and cons of investing in cryptocurrencies, it is essential to establish a clear definition of what cryptocurrencies are.

Cryptocurrencies can be defined as digital or virtual currencies that utilize cryptography for secure transactions and control the creation of additional units. Unlike traditional fiat currencies issued by central banks, cryptocurrencies are decentralized and operate on distributed ledger technology known as the blockchain.

The blockchain serves as a transparent and immutable ledger that records all transactions made with a particular cryptocurrency. This technology ensures the integrity and security of cryptocurrency transactions, eliminating the need for intermediaries such as banks.

Cryptocurrencies are typically based on cryptographic algorithms that govern their creation and transfer. They often operate independently of any central authority, allowing for peer-to-peer transactions that bypass traditional financial institutions.

Bitcoin, created by an anonymous individual or group known as Satoshi Nakamoto in 2009, was the first and most well-known cryptocurrency. However, the success and proliferation of Bitcoin paved the way for the creation of numerous other cryptocurrencies, collectively referred to as altcoins.

Altcoins, such as Ethereum, Ripple, Litecoin, and many more, have introduced innovative features and functionalities beyond the scope of Bitcoin. These cryptocurrencies often serve different purposes, ranging from digital currencies for everyday transactions to platforms for smart contracts and decentralized applications.

Investing in cryptocurrencies involves acquiring these digital assets with the expectation of generating a financial return over time. The volatility and potential for high returns in the cryptocurrency market have attracted both individual and institutional investors, driving significant interest and investment activity.

However, investing in cryptocurrencies also carries risks and challenges that must be carefully considered. Throughout this book, we will explore these pros and cons in detail, providing you with a comprehensive understanding of the opportunities and pitfalls associated with investing in cryptocurrencies.

1.2 Overview of the Cryptocurrency Market

The cryptocurrency market has experienced remarkable growth and evolution since the inception of Bitcoin. In this section, we will provide an overview of the cryptocurrency market, highlighting its size, key players, and notable trends.

The cryptocurrency market is a dynamic and fast-paced environment, characterized by a wide range of digital assets and trading platforms. As of [current year], the market capitalization of cryptocurrencies has surpassed [total market cap] billion dollars, attracting the attention of investors, traders, and enthusiasts worldwide.

One of the significant features of the cryptocurrency market is its decentralized nature. Unlike traditional financial markets, where central authorities govern and regulate transactions, cryptocurrencies operate on a peer-to-peer basis. This decentralized structure offers participants greater control over their financial assets and transactions, fostering a sense of financial autonomy and empowerment.

Bitcoin remains the most dominant cryptocurrency in terms of market capitalization and recognition. However, it is important to note that the market has witnessed the emergence of numerous altcoins, each with its unique features and use cases. Ethereum, for instance, introduced the concept of smart contracts, enabling the development of decentralized applications (DApps) on its blockchain.

The cryptocurrency market is driven by various factors, including technological advancements, regulatory developments, market sentiment, and investor demand. The market is highly volatile, with prices experiencing significant fluctuations within short periods. This volatility, while offering potential for substantial returns, also poses risks and challenges for investors.

Cryptocurrency exchanges serve as the primary platforms for buying, selling, and trading digital assets. These exchanges provide a marketplace where participants can exchange one cryptocurrency for another or convert cryptocurrencies into traditional fiat currencies. Well-known exchanges include Binance, Coinbase, Kraken, and Bitfinex, among others.

Furthermore, the cryptocurrency market has witnessed increased institutional participation in recent years. Traditional financial institutions, hedge funds, and asset management firms have started recognizing the potential of cryptocurrencies as an investment asset class. The introduction of regulated investment vehicles, such as cryptocurrency exchange-traded funds (ETFs) and futures contracts, has facilitated broader institutional access to the market.

While the cryptocurrency market offers lucrative opportunities, it is not without challenges. Regulatory uncertainties, security risks, market manipulation, and technological limitations are some of the concerns that investors must navigate. Understanding these dynamics is crucial for making informed investment decisions and managing risks effectively.

In the upcoming chapters, we will delve into the specific pros and cons of investing in cryptocurrencies, exploring the potential for high returns, the decentralization aspect, diversification benefits, as well as the risks associated with market volatility, lack of intrinsic value, regulatory challenges, and more.

1.3 Purpose of the Book

The purpose of this book is to provide readers with a comprehensive exploration of the pros and cons of investing in cryptocurrencies. By delving into the various aspects of cryptocurrency investments, we aim to equip readers with the knowledge and insights necessary to make informed decisions in this dynamic and evolving market.

Investing in cryptocurrencies can be a complex endeavor, requiring an understanding of the technology, market trends, risk management strategies, and regulatory considerations. This book aims to demystify the world of cryptocurrencies and provide a balanced view of the potential benefits and drawbacks associated with investing in this asset class.

The book will delve into the advantages of investing in cryptocurrencies, such as the potential for high returns, decentralization, and portfolio diversification. We will explore real-world success stories and examine how cryptocurrencies have disrupted traditional financial systems, providing individuals with greater financial autonomy.

However, we will not shy away from discussing the cons and challenges of investing in cryptocurrencies. Volatility, market risks, lack of intrinsic value, regulatory uncertainties, and security concerns are among the aspects that demand careful consideration. By understanding the potential pitfalls, readers can navigate the market with a more realistic perspective and make informed investment decisions.

Throughout the book, we will discuss investment strategies tailored for cryptocurrencies, delve into evaluating cryptocurrency projects, and provide guidance on security measures and legal considerations. We will also examine future trends and challenges that may impact the cryptocurrency landscape, empowering readers to stay ahead of the curve.

It is important to note that this book does not provide financial advice or guarantee investment success. Rather, it serves as a comprehensive guide to help readers understand the complexities of the cryptocurrency market and evaluate the potential risks and rewards associated with investing in cryptocurrencies.

By the end of this book, readers will have a solid foundation to navigate the world of cryptocurrencies, armed with knowledge, insights, and a well-rounded perspective. Whether you are a novice investor or a seasoned trader, this book aims to be a valuable resource in your journey to explore the world of cryptocurrency investments.

Chapter 2: Understanding Cryptocurrencies

2.1 History and Evolution of Cryptocurrencies

Cryptocurrencies have a fascinating history that traces back to the early days of computer science and cryptography. In this chapter, we will explore the key milestones and developments that led to the creation and evolution of cryptocurrencies.

The concept of cryptocurrencies can be traced back to the 1980s when researchers and cryptographers began exploring the idea of creating digital cash. In 1983, an American cryptographer named David Chaum introduced the concept of "eCash," a digital currency that aimed to provide secure and private transactions. Although eCash never gained mainstream adoption, it laid the groundwork for future advancements in digital currency technology.

A major breakthrough came in 2008 when an individual or group operating under the pseudonym Satoshi Nakamoto published a whitepaper titled "Bitcoin: A Peer-to-Peer Electronic Cash System." This whitepaper introduced Bitcoin, the world's first decentralized cryptocurrency, and the underlying technology known as blockchain.

In 2009, the Bitcoin network was launched, marking the birth of cryptocurrencies as we know them today. Bitcoin revolutionized the financial landscape by enabling peer-to-peer transactions without the need for intermediaries. It introduced the concept of mining, where participants solve complex mathematical problems to validate and secure transactions on the blockchain.

The success and growing popularity of Bitcoin paved the way for the development of other cryptocurrencies, often referred to as altcoins. In

2011, Litecoin was introduced as a "lite" version of Bitcoin, offering faster transaction confirmation times and a different hashing algorithm. Ethereum, launched in 2015 by Vitalik Buterin, introduced smart contracts, enabling the development of decentralized applications (DApps) on its blockchain.

Since then, thousands of cryptocurrencies have been created, each with its unique features, use cases, and underlying technologies. Ripple (XRP), Bitcoin Cash (BCH), Cardano (ADA), and many others have gained significant traction and market capitalization, contributing to the diversification of the cryptocurrency ecosystem.

The evolution of cryptocurrencies has also been accompanied by advancements in blockchain technology. Different consensus mechanisms, such as Proof-of-Work (PoW) and Proof-of-Stake (PoS), have been developed to secure and validate transactions on various blockchain networks. Additionally, the introduction of second-layer solutions, like the Lightning Network for Bitcoin, aims to enhance scalability and transaction speed.

The impact of cryptocurrencies has extended beyond the financial realm. Blockchain technology has found applications in various industries, including supply chain management, healthcare, voting systems, and more. The potential for decentralized and transparent systems has attracted attention from businesses, governments, and technologists seeking innovative solutions.

As cryptocurrencies continue to evolve, so do the regulatory frameworks surrounding them. Governments and financial institutions have been grappling with the challenges of regulating this nascent asset class, addressing concerns related to money laundering, tax evasion, and consumer protection. Regulatory developments have varied across countries, with some embracing cryptocurrencies and blockchain technology while others imposing stricter regulations.

Understanding the history and evolution of cryptocurrencies provides valuable context for evaluating their potential as investment assets. In the next chapter, we will explore blockchain technology and its significance in enabling the functioning of cryptocurrencies.

2.2 Blockchain Technology and Its Significance

Blockchain technology is at the core of cryptocurrencies, revolutionizing the way transactions are recorded and verified. In this section, we will delve into the workings of blockchain technology and explore its significance in enabling the functioning of cryptocurrencies.

At its essence, a blockchain is a decentralized and immutable ledger that records transactions in a chronological and transparent manner. It operates on a distributed network of computers, known as nodes, which collectively maintain and validate the blockchain's integrity.

The fundamental concept of blockchain revolves around the creation of blocks that contain batches of transactions. Each block is linked to the previous one through a cryptographic hash function, forming a chain of blocks. This structure ensures that altering any data in a block would require changing all subsequent blocks, making the blockchain resistant to tampering and fraud.

The decentralized nature of blockchain eliminates the need for a central authority, such as a bank, to validate and authorize transactions. Instead, transactions are validated by network participants, known as miners or validators, who compete to solve complex mathematical puzzles. Once a block is validated, it is added to the blockchain, becoming a permanent and transparent record of the transaction history.

The significance of blockchain technology lies in its ability to provide transparency, security, and immutability. By distributing the ledger across multiple nodes, blockchain ensures that no single entity can control or manipulate the data. This transparency fosters trust among participants, as anyone can verify and audit the transactions recorded on the blockchain.

Furthermore, the cryptographic nature of blockchain technology enhances the security of transactions. Each transaction is secured with a digital signature, making it nearly impossible for unauthorized parties to modify or forge transactions. Additionally, the decentralized nature of the blockchain makes it highly resilient to attacks, as compromising a single node does not affect the entire network.

Blockchain technology has the potential to revolutionize various industries beyond cryptocurrencies. Its applications extend to supply chain management, healthcare records, identity verification, intellectual property rights, and more. By providing a secure and transparent platform for storing and sharing data, blockchain has the potential to streamline processes, reduce fraud, and enhance efficiency in various sectors.

In the context of cryptocurrencies, blockchain technology enables the secure and decentralized transfer of digital assets. It ensures that transactions are recorded accurately and cannot be reversed or tampered with. Additionally, the transparency of the blockchain allows participants to track the flow of funds and verify the integrity of the transactions.

As cryptocurrencies continue to gain traction, advancements in blockchain technology aim to address its limitations. Issues such as scalability, energy consumption, and interoperability are being actively researched and developed to enhance the efficiency and usability of blockchain networks.

Understanding blockchain technology is crucial for comprehending the underlying mechanisms of cryptocurrencies. In the next chapter, we will explore popular cryptocurrencies and their features, providing insights into the diverse ecosystem of digital assets.

2.3 Popular Cryptocurrencies and Their Features

The cryptocurrency ecosystem is vast and diverse, with numerous digital assets serving different purposes and offering unique features. In this section, we will explore some of the most popular cryptocurrencies and delve into their distinctive characteristics.

1. Bitcoin (BTC): Bitcoin, created by Satoshi Nakamoto, is the pioneering cryptocurrency and the largest by market capitalization. It operates on a decentralized network and serves as a digital store of value and medium of exchange. Bitcoin introduced the concept of mining, where participants validate transactions and secure the network through computational power. Its key features include scarcity, transparency, and the ability to facilitate peer-to-peer transactions without intermediaries.
2. Ethereum (ETH): Ethereum is more than just a cryptocurrency; it is a decentralized platform for developing smart contracts and decentralized applications (DApps). Created by Vitalik Buterin, Ethereum introduced the concept of programmable blockchain, enabling developers to build and deploy applications on its network. Ethereum's native currency, Ether (ETH), is used to facilitate transactions and pay for computational power on the platform. Its features include smart contracts, token creation, and the ability to execute complex decentralized applications.
3. Ripple (XRP): Ripple is a digital payment protocol designed for fast and low-cost international money transfers. Unlike most cryptocurrencies, Ripple does not rely on mining. Instead, it operates on a consensus algorithm known as the

Ripple Protocol Consensus Algorithm (RPCA). Ripple's native currency, XRP, serves as a bridge currency for facilitating cross-border transactions. Key features of Ripple include fast transaction settlement times, scalability, and its focus on partnerships with financial institutions.

4. Litecoin (LTC): Litecoin is often referred to as the "silver" to Bitcoin's "gold." Created by Charlie Lee, Litecoin is a peer-to-peer cryptocurrency that shares many similarities with Bitcoin. However, it offers faster transaction confirmation times and uses a different hashing algorithm called Scrypt. Litecoin aims to provide a more efficient and accessible payment option while maintaining the core principles of decentralization and security.
5. Cardano (ADA): Cardano is a blockchain platform that aims to provide a secure and scalable infrastructure for the development of decentralized applications and smart contracts. It focuses on research-driven development and emphasizes principles such as peer review and formal verification. Cardano's native currency, ADA, is used for transaction settlement and participation in the platform's proof-of-stake consensus mechanism. Notable features of Cardano include its focus on security, sustainability, and the ability to upgrade the blockchain through soft forks.

These are just a few examples of popular cryptocurrencies in the market, each with its unique features and value propositions. Other notable cryptocurrencies include Bitcoin Cash (BCH), Binance Coin (BNB), Polkadot (DOT), and Chainlink (LINK), among many others.

When evaluating cryptocurrencies, factors to consider include their use cases, underlying technology, team behind the project, community support, and market demand. Additionally, it is important to assess the regulatory landscape and potential risks associated with each cryptocurrency.

Understanding the features and diversity within the cryptocurrency ecosystem enables investors to make informed decisions and identify cryptocurrencies that align with their investment goals and risk tolerance.

Chapter 3: Pros of Investing in Cryptocurrencies

3.1 Potential for High Returns

One of the primary attractions of investing in cryptocurrencies is the potential for high returns. The volatile nature of the cryptocurrency market has led to significant price fluctuations, which, for some investors, have translated into substantial profits. In this section, we will explore the factors that contribute to the potential for high returns in cryptocurrency investments.

1. Early-stage Investment Opportunities: Cryptocurrencies offer the opportunity to invest in early-stage projects with significant growth potential. Many successful cryptocurrencies, such as Bitcoin and Ethereum, experienced substantial price appreciation in their early years. Investing in promising projects at an early stage allows investors to benefit from the growth of the cryptocurrency as it gains popularity and adoption.
2. Market Volatility: The cryptocurrency market is known for its high volatility, characterized by rapid price movements within short periods. While volatility may pose risks, it also presents opportunities for significant returns. Traders and investors who can effectively navigate and capitalize on market trends and price swings may generate substantial profits.
3. Limited Supply and Scarcity: Certain cryptocurrencies, such as Bitcoin, have a limited supply, which contributes to their value proposition. Bitcoin, for instance, has a maximum supply of 21 million coins. The scarcity of these digital assets can drive up demand and potentially lead to price

appreciation over time. This scarcity factor, combined with growing adoption, has historically been a significant driver of high returns in cryptocurrencies.

4. Disruption of Traditional Financial Systems: Cryptocurrencies have the potential to disrupt traditional financial systems and revolutionize various industries. As cryptocurrencies gain mainstream acceptance and adoption, they can challenge the dominance of centralized financial institutions and payment systems. This disruption can create opportunities for investors who position themselves early in the transition to decentralized financial ecosystems.
5. Global Accessibility: Cryptocurrencies provide global accessibility, allowing individuals from different parts of the world to participate in the digital economy. This accessibility breaks down barriers to entry, enabling a broader pool of investors to engage in cryptocurrency trading and investment. The democratization of investment opportunities can contribute to increased demand and, potentially, higher returns.

It is important to note that investing in cryptocurrencies also carries inherent risks. The high volatility of the market can lead to significant losses, and regulatory uncertainties and security concerns pose additional challenges. Therefore, it is crucial for investors to conduct thorough research, develop risk management strategies, and diversify their investment portfolios.

While the potential for high returns is an appealing aspect of investing in cryptocurrencies, it is essential to approach these investments with caution and a long-term perspective. Understanding the market dynamics, staying informed about the latest developments, and maintaining a disciplined investment approach can help investors navigate the potential risks and maximize the opportunities for returns.

3.1.1 Historical Price Appreciation of Cryptocurrencies

One of the notable aspects of investing in cryptocurrencies is the historical price appreciation that some digital assets have experienced. While past performance is not indicative of future results, examining the price appreciation of cryptocurrencies can provide insights into their potential for high returns. In this subsection, we will explore the historical price appreciation of several prominent cryptocurrencies.

1. Bitcoin (BTC): Bitcoin, being the first and largest cryptocurrency, has showcased remarkable price appreciation since its inception. In its early days, Bitcoin had a relatively low value, with prices less than a cent per coin. However, over time, Bitcoin gained significant attention and experienced remarkable growth. The most notable surge occurred in late 2017, when Bitcoin reached an all-time high price of nearly $20,000. Although Bitcoin's price has experienced volatility since then, it has maintained a higher value compared to its early years.
2. Ethereum (ETH): Ethereum has also witnessed notable price appreciation throughout its existence. Since its launch in 2015, Ethereum has gone through several price cycles. The most significant surge occurred in early 2021 when the price of Ethereum reached an all-time high of over $4,000. The popularity of Ethereum's blockchain platform, along with its role in facilitating decentralized applications and smart contracts, has contributed to its price growth.
3. Ripple (XRP): Ripple's native cryptocurrency, XRP, has also experienced significant price movements over the years. XRP reached its peak price in early 2018 when it surged to over $3. However, it is worth noting that Ripple's price performance has been subject to regulatory scrutiny and legal challenges, which have impacted its value.

4. Litecoin (LTC): Litecoin has had its share of notable price appreciation, particularly during bull market cycles. In late 2017, Litecoin reached its all-time high of over $350. Although Litecoin's price has fluctuated since then, it has maintained a relatively higher value compared to its early years.
5. Other Cryptocurrencies: Beyond the aforementioned cryptocurrencies, numerous other digital assets have showcased substantial price appreciation. For instance, Binance Coin (BNB), Cardano (ADA), and Polkadot (DOT) have witnessed significant growth during certain market cycles.

It is crucial to emphasize that the cryptocurrency market is highly volatile, and price appreciation is not guaranteed. Investors should exercise caution and conduct thorough research before making investment decisions. Additionally, diversification and risk management strategies are essential to navigate the market's inherent volatility.

While historical price appreciation can be enticing, it is important to approach cryptocurrency investments with a long-term perspective, considering factors such as the underlying technology, project fundamentals, market dynamics, and regulatory environment. Investing in cryptocurrencies should be based on a thorough analysis of the risks and rewards involved.

3.1.2 Success Stories of Early Cryptocurrency Investors

The cryptocurrency market has witnessed several success stories of early investors who have reaped significant returns on their investments. While these stories represent exceptional cases and should not be taken as a guarantee of future success, they provide insights into the potential rewards of investing in cryptocurrencies. In this subsection, we will explore some notable success stories of early cryptocurrency investors.

1. The Winklevoss Twins: Cameron and Tyler Winklevoss, known for their involvement in the early development of Facebook, made a significant investment in Bitcoin in 2013. They purchased approximately 120,000 BTC, which was worth around $11 million at the time. The value of their investment soared as the price of Bitcoin surged, and by 2017, their Bitcoin holdings were worth over $1 billion.
2. Erik Finman: Erik Finman, a teenager at the time, became a millionaire through his early investment in Bitcoin. In 2011, at the age of 12, he used a $1,000 gift from his grandmother to purchase Bitcoin when it was trading around $12 per coin. By 2017, the value of his Bitcoin holdings surpassed $4 million. Finman's story gained media attention, highlighting the potential for substantial returns in the cryptocurrency market.
3. Charlie Shrem: Charlie Shrem, an early Bitcoin advocate and entrepreneur, is another notable success story. In 2011, he co-founded BitInstant, a Bitcoin exchange, and processing company. Shrem's involvement in the early Bitcoin ecosystem led to significant financial success. Although his journey faced legal challenges later on, his early investments and contributions to the Bitcoin industry played a role in his financial success.
4. Gavin Andresen: Gavin Andresen, a software developer, was heavily involved in the early development of Bitcoin. As one of the key contributors to the Bitcoin codebase, Andresen was appointed as the lead developer of the Bitcoin project by Satoshi Nakamoto. He received a substantial number of Bitcoins as part of his contributions. While the exact value of

his holdings is unknown, his involvement in the early days of Bitcoin positioned him for potential significant returns.

These success stories highlight the immense potential for substantial returns in the cryptocurrency market. However, it is crucial to note that investing in cryptocurrencies comes with risks, and individual outcomes may vary. Market volatility, regulatory uncertainties, and technological challenges are factors that investors must consider and carefully assess.

Additionally, success stories tend to gain attention due to their exceptional nature. They should not overshadow the importance of thorough research, risk management, and a long-term investment approach. Investing in cryptocurrencies requires a comprehensive understanding of the market, diligent decision-making, and diversification across different assets.

3.2 Decentralization and Financial Freedom

One of the fundamental principles of cryptocurrencies is their decentralized nature, which offers the potential for financial autonomy and freedom. In this section, we will explore the advantages of decentralization and how it contributes to financial freedom in the context of investing in cryptocurrencies.

1. Removal of Intermediaries: Traditional financial systems often rely on intermediaries such as banks, payment processors, and clearinghouses. These intermediaries can introduce inefficiencies, delays, and additional costs into financial transactions. Cryptocurrencies, on the other hand, operate on decentralized networks, allowing direct peer-to-peer transactions without the need for intermediaries. This removal of intermediaries streamlines financial processes and can potentially reduce transaction costs, enabling individuals

to have greater control over their funds.

2. Financial Inclusion: Decentralized cryptocurrencies have the potential to promote financial inclusion by providing access to financial services to individuals who are underserved by traditional banking systems. Many people worldwide, especially in developing countries, lack access to basic banking services. Cryptocurrencies allow anyone with internet access to participate in the global financial ecosystem, empowering individuals to store, transfer, and invest their assets without relying on traditional financial institutions. This increased accessibility can foster economic growth and empower individuals to take control of their financial futures.
3. Protection against Government Control and Inflation: In some regions, governments exercise strict control over their national currencies, leading to issues such as capital controls, inflation, and economic instability. Cryptocurrencies offer an alternative that operates independently of any government or central authority. The decentralized nature of cryptocurrencies, coupled with features like limited supply and transparency, provides a potential hedge against inflation and government interference. Investors who seek to diversify their portfolios and protect their wealth from the risks associated with traditional fiat currencies may find cryptocurrencies appealing.
4. Ownership and Control of Assets: When investing in cryptocurrencies, investors have direct ownership and control over their digital assets. Unlike traditional financial systems, where assets are often held and managed by intermediaries, cryptocurrencies enable individuals to hold and manage their funds using digital wallets and private keys. This ownership and control offer increased security and flexibility, as

individuals are not reliant on third parties to safeguard their assets. It also reduces the risk of asset seizure or freezing by authorities.

5. Global Accessibility and Borderless Transactions: Cryptocurrencies transcend geographical boundaries, allowing individuals to engage in cross-border transactions easily. Traditional financial systems often impose restrictions and fees on international transfers, making them cumbersome and expensive. Cryptocurrencies facilitate fast, low-cost, and borderless transactions, eliminating many of the barriers associated with cross-border payments. This global accessibility opens up opportunities for international trade, remittances, and investment activities on a global scale.

While the advantages of decentralization and financial freedom are appealing, it is important to acknowledge that the cryptocurrency market is still evolving, and regulatory frameworks are being developed to address potential risks. Investors should exercise caution, conduct thorough research, and understand the legal and regulatory environment surrounding cryptocurrencies in their respective jurisdictions.

3.2.1 Disruption of Traditional Financial Systems

Cryptocurrencies have the potential to disrupt traditional financial systems, offering alternative solutions that challenge the existing centralized infrastructure. In this subsection, we will explore how cryptocurrencies can disrupt traditional financial systems and the advantages that arise from this disruption.

1. Elimination of Middlemen: Traditional financial systems often rely on intermediaries, such as banks, to facilitate transactions and maintain records. These intermediaries can

introduce delays, fees, and complexities into financial processes. Cryptocurrencies, operating on decentralized networks like blockchain, enable peer-to-peer transactions without the need for intermediaries. This direct interaction between participants reduces costs, speeds up transactions, and enhances efficiency.

2. Lower Transaction Costs: Cryptocurrencies can significantly reduce transaction costs compared to traditional financial systems. Traditional payment methods involve fees for processing, currency conversion, and cross-border transfers. Cryptocurrencies eliminate or minimize many of these costs, allowing individuals to transact with lower fees. This cost reduction can benefit individuals, businesses, and even the unbanked population, facilitating financial inclusion and fostering economic growth.
3. Enhanced Security and Privacy: Cryptocurrencies utilize cryptographic techniques to secure transactions and protect user identities. Blockchain technology ensures transparency, immutability, and resistance to fraud. Unlike traditional financial systems, which can be vulnerable to cyber attacks and data breaches, cryptocurrencies provide a higher level of security. Additionally, cryptocurrencies offer varying levels of privacy, empowering individuals to control their financial information and protect their identities.
4. Accessibility to Global Markets: Traditional financial systems often restrict access to global markets, particularly for individuals in developing countries or regions with limited banking infrastructure. Cryptocurrencies, being decentralized and accessible through the internet, enable individuals from anywhere in the world to participate in global financial markets. This accessibility opens up opportunities for investment, entrepreneurship, and

economic empowerment on a global scale.

5. Democratization of Fundraising: Cryptocurrencies have introduced new models of fundraising, such as Initial Coin Offerings (ICOs) and Initial Exchange Offerings (IEOs). These models allow projects and startups to raise funds directly from the public, bypassing the traditional venture capital and investment banking channels. This democratization of fundraising provides opportunities for innovative projects to access capital and disrupt established industries.
6. Financial Sovereignty: Cryptocurrencies offer individuals greater financial sovereignty, allowing them to have full control over their assets and transactions. In traditional financial systems, individuals must rely on financial institutions and governments for permission to access and use their funds. Cryptocurrencies empower individuals with the ability to transact and store value independently, free from centralized control. This financial sovereignty aligns with the principles of decentralization and personal freedom.

While the disruption of traditional financial systems brings numerous advantages, it also poses challenges and regulatory considerations. Governments and financial institutions are adapting to the rise of cryptocurrencies, seeking to strike a balance between innovation and consumer protection. Investors must be aware of the evolving regulatory landscape and exercise due diligence in navigating the cryptocurrency market.

3.2.2 Peer-to-Peer Transactions and Reduced Intermediaries

One of the key advantages of investing in cryptocurrencies is the ability to engage in peer-to-peer transactions, bypassing traditional intermediaries. In this subsection, we will explore the benefits of peer-to-peer transactions and the reduction of intermediaries in the cryptocurrency ecosystem.

1. Direct Ownership and Control: Cryptocurrencies enable individuals to have direct ownership and control over their digital assets. Through the use of digital wallets and private keys, investors can securely store and manage their cryptocurrencies without relying on third-party custodians. This direct control eliminates the need for intermediaries, such as banks or brokers, reducing the associated fees and potential risks.
2. Increased Transaction Speed: Traditional financial transactions often involve multiple intermediaries, leading to delays in settlement and clearance. Cryptocurrencies facilitate near-instantaneous transactions, especially within the same blockchain network. By removing intermediaries, peer-to-peer transactions occur directly between the transacting parties, resulting in faster settlement times. This speed can be particularly beneficial for cross-border transactions, which typically require multiple intermediaries and can take days to complete using traditional systems.
3. Cost Reduction: Reducing intermediaries in financial transactions can lead to cost savings. Traditional banking systems often involve fees for various services, including wire transfers, currency conversions, and account maintenance. Cryptocurrencies minimize or eliminate these fees, allowing users to send and receive funds at a fraction of the cost associated with traditional methods. Additionally, peer-to-peer transactions can lower costs by removing the need for intermediaries to facilitate and validate transactions.
4. Enhanced Privacy: Cryptocurrencies provide a level of privacy and pseudonymity, allowing users to transact without

revealing their real-world identities. While transactions are recorded on a public blockchain, the actual identities behind the transactions are often represented by cryptographic addresses. This privacy feature can be appealing for individuals who value financial confidentiality and seek to protect their transactional information.

5. Global Accessibility: The peer-to-peer nature of cryptocurrencies enables global accessibility to financial services. Traditional banking systems may have limitations, especially for individuals without access to a bank account or those in regions with underdeveloped financial infrastructure. Cryptocurrencies overcome these barriers, allowing anyone with an internet connection to participate in the global financial ecosystem. This inclusivity fosters financial empowerment and opens up economic opportunities for individuals worldwide.
6. Disintermediation of Financial Services: Cryptocurrencies have the potential to disrupt and disintermediate various financial services. For example, decentralized finance (DeFi) platforms built on blockchain technology enable peer-to-peer lending, borrowing, and trading without the need for traditional financial intermediaries. These platforms provide access to financial services directly to users, creating a more inclusive and efficient financial system.

By enabling peer-to-peer transactions and reducing intermediaries, cryptocurrencies offer individuals greater control over their financial activities, faster transactions, reduced costs, enhanced privacy, and global accessibility. However, it is important to consider the potential risks and challenges associated with these advantages, such as regulatory concerns, technological limitations, and the need for responsible financial management.

3.2.3 Accessibility to Unbanked Populations

One of the significant advantages of cryptocurrencies is their potential to provide financial access and inclusion to unbanked populations. In this subsection, we will explore how cryptocurrencies can bridge the gap for individuals who lack access to traditional banking services.

1. Financial Inclusion: Cryptocurrencies have the potential to bring financial services to the unbanked, who are typically excluded from the traditional banking system. According to the World Bank, around 1.7 billion adults worldwide remain unbanked, lacking access to basic financial services. Cryptocurrencies offer an alternative means for these individuals to store, transfer, and invest their assets. With just a smartphone and internet access, unbanked populations can participate in the global financial ecosystem and experience financial inclusion.
2. Lower Barriers to Entry: Traditional banking systems often have stringent requirements and documentation procedures that make it challenging for individuals to open bank accounts. This creates barriers to accessing financial services, especially for those without official identification or proof of residence. Cryptocurrencies, however, do not require the same level of documentation, allowing individuals to create digital wallets and engage in transactions with minimal prerequisites. This lower barrier to entry empowers unbanked populations to join the digital economy and access financial tools.
3. Cross-Border Transactions and Remittances: For individuals in developing countries who rely on remittances from abroad, cryptocurrencies offer a more efficient and cost-effective solution. Traditional remittance services often involve high fees and lengthy processing times. Cryptocurrencies facilitate

borderless transactions, allowing users to send and receive funds internationally at a lower cost and faster speed. This capability can significantly benefit unbanked populations who heavily rely on remittances for their livelihoods.

4. Microtransactions and Microlending: Cryptocurrencies enable microtransactions, which are particularly beneficial for unbanked populations with low-income levels. With cryptocurrencies, individuals can transact in tiny fractions, making it feasible to engage in micro-commerce and access goods and services that were previously inaccessible. Furthermore, cryptocurrencies open up opportunities for microlending, where individuals can borrow or lend small amounts of funds without relying on traditional banking systems. This empowers unbanked individuals to engage in entrepreneurial activities and improve their economic conditions.
5. Security and Trust: For unbanked populations, security and trust in financial transactions can be major concerns. Cryptocurrencies utilize cryptographic techniques and decentralized networks to secure transactions and protect user data. The transparent and immutable nature of blockchain technology helps build trust and reduce the risk of fraud. By providing a secure and reliable financial infrastructure, cryptocurrencies offer unbanked populations a viable alternative to traditional banking systems.
6. Financial Empowerment: By enabling access to financial services, cryptocurrencies provide unbanked populations with greater control over their financial lives. They can save, invest, and participate in economic activities without relying on intermediaries or facing the limitations imposed by the traditional banking system. This financial empowerment can lead to improved economic conditions, increased financial

literacy, and enhanced opportunities for socio-economic growth.

While cryptocurrencies offer significant potential for financial inclusion, it is important to address the challenges and considerations associated with their adoption. Factors such as technological literacy, infrastructure limitations, and regulatory frameworks need to be carefully navigated to ensure the responsible and effective use of cryptocurrencies for unbanked populations.

3.3 Diversification and Portfolio Growth

Diversification is a commonly employed strategy in investment portfolios to reduce risk and maximize potential returns. In this section, we will explore how investing in cryptocurrencies can contribute to portfolio diversification and potentially foster portfolio growth.

1. Low Correlation with Traditional Assets: Cryptocurrencies have exhibited low correlation with traditional asset classes, such as stocks, bonds, and commodities. This means that their price movements often occur independently or with minimal correlation to the performance of traditional investments. By adding cryptocurrencies to an investment portfolio, investors can potentially reduce the overall risk and volatility of their portfolio. Cryptocurrencies' unique market dynamics can provide diversification benefits by acting as a separate asset class with its own risk and return characteristics.
2. Potential High Returns: Cryptocurrencies have demonstrated the potential for significant price appreciation over relatively short periods. While this potential for high returns comes with increased volatility and risk, it also

presents an opportunity for portfolio growth. By allocating a portion of an investment portfolio to cryptocurrencies, investors may position themselves to benefit from the growth of the cryptocurrency market and potentially outperform traditional asset classes. It is worth noting that cryptocurrency investments should be approached with caution, and thorough research and risk management strategies should be employed.

3. Exposure to Technological Innovations: Investing in cryptocurrencies provides exposure to disruptive technologies, such as blockchain and decentralized applications (dApps). These technologies have the potential to revolutionize various industries, including finance, supply chain management, and healthcare. By including cryptocurrencies in a portfolio, investors can participate in the growth and adoption of these innovative technologies, which may have long-term implications for economic and social development.
4. Access to Emerging Markets: Cryptocurrencies offer access to emerging markets that may be challenging to access through traditional investment vehicles. Many cryptocurrencies are global in nature and can be transacted without geographical limitations. This provides investors with an opportunity to invest in projects and economies that are experiencing rapid growth and technological advancements. Exposure to emerging markets through cryptocurrencies can diversify a portfolio and potentially generate higher returns compared to investments limited to established markets.
5. Liquidity and Trading Opportunities: Cryptocurrency markets are known for their liquidity and trading opportunities. The 24/7 availability and high trading volumes of major cryptocurrencies enable investors to enter

and exit positions with relative ease. This liquidity can be particularly advantageous for active traders and investors who seek short-term opportunities. By incorporating cryptocurrencies into a portfolio, investors can tap into these dynamic markets and potentially benefit from price fluctuations and trading strategies.

6. Innovation and Early Adoption: Cryptocurrencies represent an innovative space where new projects, protocols, and technologies emerge regularly. Investing in cryptocurrencies allows investors to be part of this ecosystem and potentially identify promising projects at an early stage. Early adoption of successful cryptocurrencies or blockchain-based platforms can result in substantial returns for investors. However, it is crucial to conduct thorough research and due diligence to evaluate the viability and potential risks associated with investing in emerging projects.

By including cryptocurrencies in an investment portfolio, investors can potentially enhance diversification, gain exposure to technological innovations, access emerging markets, take advantage of liquidity, and participate in the potential growth of the cryptocurrency ecosystem. However, it is important to remember that cryptocurrency investments come with inherent risks, including market volatility, regulatory uncertainties, and technological challenges. Investors should carefully assess their risk tolerance and consider consulting with financial professionals before making investment decisions.

3.3.1 Correlation with Traditional Assets

When constructing an investment portfolio, one of the key considerations is the correlation between different assets. In this subsection, we will explore the correlation between cryptocurrencies and traditional assets, highlighting the potential benefits of including cryptocurrencies in a diversified portfolio.

1. Low Correlation: Cryptocurrencies, such as Bitcoin and Ethereum, have exhibited low correlation with traditional asset classes, such as stocks, bonds, and commodities. This means that the price movements of cryptocurrencies often occur independently or have minimal correlation with the performance of traditional investments. By including cryptocurrencies in a portfolio, investors can potentially reduce the overall risk and volatility of their portfolio through diversification. During periods of market turbulence or economic downturns, the low correlation with traditional assets may provide a hedge against losses in other parts of the portfolio.
2. Potential for Uncorrelated Returns: The low correlation between cryptocurrencies and traditional assets can also lead to the potential for uncorrelated returns. When cryptocurrencies experience price movements that are not closely tied to traditional markets, they can provide an opportunity for portfolio growth even when other asset classes are performing differently. This potential for uncorrelated returns can enhance the overall risk-adjusted performance of a diversified investment portfolio.
3. Hedge Against Inflation and Currency Risks: Cryptocurrencies, particularly those with limited supply, have gained attention as a potential hedge against inflation and currency risks. Traditional fiat currencies can lose value over time due to factors such as government policies, economic instability, and inflationary pressures. Cryptocurrencies, on the other hand, often have built-in mechanisms to limit supply, such as Bitcoin's fixed maximum

supply of 21 million coins. As a result, cryptocurrencies may retain or increase their value during periods of currency depreciation or inflation, providing a potential hedge against such risks.

4. Exposure to Digital Economy: Cryptocurrencies represent a gateway to the digital economy, which is becoming increasingly important in today's interconnected world. As technology continues to shape various industries, investing in cryptocurrencies can provide exposure to the growth and adoption of digital assets, blockchain technology, and decentralized applications. By including cryptocurrencies in a portfolio, investors position themselves to benefit from the ongoing digital transformation and potentially capitalize on the growth of digital assets.
5. Potential Alpha Generation: The unique characteristics of the cryptocurrency market, such as its high volatility and rapid price movements, can create opportunities for alpha generation. Skilled investors and active traders can employ strategies to capture short-term price fluctuations and generate alpha, which refers to returns that exceed the market average. By allocating a portion of a portfolio to cryptocurrencies, investors with expertise in the market can potentially generate additional returns through active management and trading strategies.

It is important to note that while including cryptocurrencies in a portfolio can provide diversification benefits, they also come with their own set of risks. Cryptocurrencies are known for their high volatility, regulatory uncertainties, and technological challenges. Therefore, investors should carefully assess their risk tolerance, conduct thorough research, and consider diversifying across multiple cryptocurrencies to mitigate specific risks associated with individual cryptocurrencies.

3.3.2 Adding a Non-Correlated Asset Class to Investment Portfolios

One of the advantages of investing in cryptocurrencies is the potential to add a non-correlated asset class to investment portfolios. In this subsection, we will explore the benefits of including cryptocurrencies as a non-correlated asset class and its impact on portfolio diversification.

1. Risk Reduction through Diversification: Diversification is a fundamental principle in portfolio management that aims to reduce risk by allocating investments across different asset classes. By adding cryptocurrencies to an investment portfolio, investors can introduce an asset class that has historically shown a low correlation with traditional investments, such as stocks and bonds. This non-correlation can help mitigate the impact of market volatility and potentially enhance risk-adjusted returns. The inclusion of non-correlated assets like cryptocurrencies can lead to more stable portfolio performance and reduce the reliance on the performance of a single asset class.
2. Potential for Enhanced Returns: The inclusion of a non-correlated asset class like cryptocurrencies offers the potential for enhanced portfolio returns. Since cryptocurrencies have shown relatively independent price movements from traditional assets, they can generate returns that are not solely dependent on the performance of the stock or bond markets. During periods of market volatility or economic downturns, the inclusion of cryptocurrencies in a portfolio can act as a potential source of returns and serve as a diversification tool to capture unique market opportunities.
3. Exposure to Alternative Investment Opportunities: Cryptocurrencies provide access to alternative investment opportunities that are not typically available through traditional financial instruments. The cryptocurrency market

offers a wide range of digital assets, including established cryptocurrencies like Bitcoin and Ethereum, as well as emerging tokens and decentralized finance (DeFi) projects. These alternative investment opportunities can provide exposure to technological innovations, disruptive business models, and new avenues of economic growth. By incorporating cryptocurrencies into an investment portfolio, investors can diversify their exposure and potentially benefit from the growth of this evolving asset class.

4. Hedge Against Systemic Risks: Including a non-correlated asset class like cryptocurrencies can serve as a hedge against systemic risks that may affect traditional financial markets. Systemic risks refer to factors that have the potential to disrupt the overall functioning of financial systems, such as economic crises, geopolitical events, or policy changes. Cryptocurrencies, with their decentralized nature and independence from traditional financial systems, may offer a level of protection during times of systemic risk. This can help cushion the impact of such events on an investment portfolio and provide a potential source of stability.
5. Portfolio Customization and Optimization: By adding cryptocurrencies as a non-correlated asset class, investors can customize and optimize their investment portfolios to align with their risk tolerance and investment objectives. The inclusion of cryptocurrencies allows for greater diversification and flexibility in portfolio construction. Investors can allocate a portion of their portfolio to cryptocurrencies based on their risk appetite and desired exposure to this unique asset class. This customization empowers investors to create portfolios that reflect their individual investment preferences and goals.

It is important to note that the inclusion of cryptocurrencies in an investment portfolio should be done with careful consideration and an understanding of the associated risks. Cryptocurrencies are known for their volatility and regulatory uncertainties, which can impact their market performance. Therefore, investors should conduct thorough research, seek professional advice, and assess their risk tolerance before allocating a portion of their portfolio to cryptocurrencies.

Chapter 4: Cons of Investing in Cryptocurrencies

4.1 Volatility and Market Risks

While investing in cryptocurrencies offers potential benefits, it also comes with a range of risks and drawbacks. In this chapter, we will explore the cons of investing in cryptocurrencies, starting with the significant volatility and market risks associated with this asset class.

1. High Price Volatility: Cryptocurrencies are known for their high price volatility, with substantial price swings occurring within short periods. The cryptocurrency market is relatively young and lacks the stability and regulation of traditional financial markets. Factors such as market sentiment, news events, regulatory developments, and technological advancements can greatly impact cryptocurrency prices. The rapid and unpredictable price movements can result in significant gains for investors but also expose them to the risk of substantial losses. It is essential to recognize and be prepared for the inherent volatility when investing in cryptocurrencies.
2. Market Manipulation: Due to the decentralized and largely unregulated nature of the cryptocurrency market, it is susceptible to market manipulation. Pump-and-dump schemes, insider trading, and price manipulation tactics can artificially inflate or deflate the prices of cryptocurrencies. These fraudulent practices can mislead investors and create an unfair trading environment. It is crucial for investors to exercise caution, conduct thorough research, and be vigilant against potential market manipulation when investing in cryptocurrencies.

3. Regulatory Uncertainty: Regulatory frameworks surrounding cryptocurrencies are still evolving in many jurisdictions. Governments and regulatory bodies worldwide are grappling with how to approach and regulate this emerging asset class. Regulatory changes or crackdowns on cryptocurrencies can have a significant impact on their prices and market liquidity. Uncertainty regarding the legal and regulatory landscape introduces additional risks and challenges for investors. It is important to stay informed about regulatory developments and be prepared for potential changes in the regulatory environment.
4. Security Risks: Investing in cryptocurrencies carries inherent security risks. While cryptocurrencies leverage advanced cryptographic techniques to secure transactions, the digital nature of these assets exposes them to cybersecurity threats. Hacking attempts, phishing attacks, and thefts from cryptocurrency exchanges are not uncommon. If proper security measures are not in place, investors can lose their funds due to security breaches. It is essential to adopt best practices for securing cryptocurrency wallets and carefully choose reputable and secure platforms for trading and storage.
5. Lack of Fundamental Valuation: Valuing cryptocurrencies can be challenging due to the absence of traditional fundamental metrics commonly used in valuing stocks or bonds. The valuation of cryptocurrencies is influenced by factors such as market sentiment, technological advancements, adoption rates, and network activity. The lack of reliable fundamental data makes it difficult to assess the intrinsic value of cryptocurrencies, which can lead to speculative pricing and increased investment risks.
6. Liquidity Risks: While major cryptocurrencies like Bitcoin

and Ethereum have established liquidity, many smaller or less popular cryptocurrencies may suffer from liquidity risks. Low trading volumes and limited market depth can result in price slippage, making it challenging to execute large transactions at desired prices. Illiquid markets also pose challenges when it comes to entering or exiting positions swiftly, potentially hindering the ability to capitalize on investment opportunities or manage risk effectively.

7. Operational and Technological Risks: Investing in cryptocurrencies requires an understanding of the underlying technology and potential operational risks. Cryptocurrencies rely on blockchain technology, which is still evolving and susceptible to technical issues, software bugs, and security vulnerabilities. Forks, system upgrades, or protocol changes can introduce uncertainties and impact the value and functionality of specific cryptocurrencies. Additionally, user error, such as losing access to private keys or forgetting passwords, can result in irreversible loss of funds. It is crucial to be aware of these operational and technological risks and take appropriate precautions when engaging with cryptocurrencies.

By acknowledging and understanding the volatility and market risks associated with cryptocurrencies, investors can make informed decisions and manage their investments effectively. Implementing risk management strategies, diversifying portfolios, staying updated on market developments, and conducting thorough research can help mitigate some of the risks involved in cryptocurrency investing.

4.1.1 Price Fluctuations and Market Instability

One of the primary drawbacks of investing in cryptocurrencies is the significant price fluctuations and market instability associated with this asset class. In this subsection, we will delve deeper into the challenges posed by price volatility and market instability.

1. High Price Volatility: Cryptocurrencies are known for their extreme price volatility. The value of cryptocurrencies can fluctuate dramatically within short periods, sometimes experiencing double-digit percentage changes in a single day. This high volatility can be attributed to various factors, including market sentiment, regulatory announcements, technological advancements, macroeconomic events, and even social media influence. The volatile nature of cryptocurrencies can result in substantial gains for investors but also exposes them to the risk of significant losses if not managed carefully.
2. Speculative Trading: The high price volatility of cryptocurrencies often attracts speculative traders who aim to profit from short-term price movements. Speculation can further contribute to increased price volatility, as traders buy and sell cryptocurrencies based on market sentiment and anticipated price trends rather than underlying fundamentals. Speculative trading can amplify price swings, making it challenging for long-term investors to navigate the market with stability and predictability.
3. Lack of Market Stability: The cryptocurrency market is relatively young and lacks the stability and regulation of traditional financial markets. It is still developing and maturing, with ongoing technological advancements, regulatory changes, and market shifts. The lack of stability can lead to significant price fluctuations and uncertainties, as the market is susceptible to external factors that can influence investor sentiment and market dynamics. The absence of established market stability can make it difficult for investors

to assess the long-term viability and sustainability of specific cryptocurrencies.

4. Market Manipulation: The decentralized and largely unregulated nature of the cryptocurrency market makes it susceptible to market manipulation. Manipulation tactics, such as pump-and-dump schemes, can artificially inflate or deflate the prices of cryptocurrencies, deceiving unsuspecting investors. Additionally, the relatively low trading volumes of some cryptocurrencies can make them more vulnerable to manipulation by influential market participants. These manipulative practices can create an unfair trading environment and undermine the integrity of the market.
5. Emotional Investing: The rapid price fluctuations and market instability in the cryptocurrency space can trigger emotional responses among investors. Fear and greed can drive impulsive decision-making, leading to irrational buying or selling behavior. Emotional investing can hinder sound investment strategies and prompt investors to make decisions based on short-term market movements rather than long-term fundamentals. It is important for investors to stay disciplined, avoid succumbing to emotional biases, and base their investment decisions on thorough analysis and research.
6. Impact on Investor Psychology: The price volatility and market instability of cryptocurrencies can have a psychological impact on investors. Sharp price declines or significant market corrections can induce fear and panic, leading some investors to sell their holdings at a loss or exit the market altogether. Conversely, periods of rapid price appreciation can generate FOMO (fear of missing out), causing investors to enter the market at inflated prices. The psychological aspect of investing in cryptocurrencies adds an additional layer of complexity and can significantly impact

investor behavior and decision-making.

It is essential for investors to carefully consider the potential impact of price fluctuations and market instability when investing in cryptocurrencies. Establishing a risk management strategy, setting realistic expectations, conducting thorough research, and maintaining a long-term investment perspective can help navigate the challenges posed by volatile markets and enhance the chances of achieving investment goals.

4.1.2 Lack of Regulations and Market Manipulation

In addition to the price fluctuations and market instability discussed earlier, another significant drawback of investing in cryptocurrencies is the lack of regulations and the potential for market manipulation. In this subsection, we will explore the challenges posed by the absence of robust regulations and the risks associated with market manipulation in the cryptocurrency market.

1. Regulatory Uncertainty: The regulatory landscape for cryptocurrencies is still evolving, with different countries and jurisdictions implementing varying degrees of regulations. The lack of consistent and comprehensive regulations can create uncertainties and challenges for investors. The absence of clear guidelines regarding cryptocurrency exchanges, initial coin offerings (ICOs), and other aspects of the cryptocurrency ecosystem can lead to confusion and potential risks. Regulatory changes or the introduction of new regulations can impact the legal status, trading activities, and market liquidity of cryptocurrencies, which can significantly affect their value and the investment landscape.
2. Market Manipulation: The decentralized and relatively unregulated nature of the cryptocurrency market makes it

susceptible to market manipulation. Market manipulation refers to practices that distort the true supply and demand dynamics, leading to artificial price movements. Manipulative activities, such as pump-and-dump schemes, wash trading, spoofing, and front-running, can mislead investors and create an unfair trading environment. The lack of robust regulations and oversight can make it easier for malicious actors to manipulate prices and take advantage of unsuspecting investors.

3. Lack of Investor Protection: Unlike traditional financial markets, the cryptocurrency market often lacks the same level of investor protection measures. Regulatory frameworks and investor protection mechanisms, such as deposit insurance and securities regulations, may not be fully applicable to cryptocurrencies. This absence of protection measures increases the risk of fraud, theft, and other malicious activities. Investors must exercise caution, conduct thorough due diligence, and choose reputable platforms and service providers to minimize the risk of falling victim to scams or fraudulent schemes.
4. Insider Trading: Due to the decentralized and global nature of cryptocurrencies, information dissemination can be challenging to regulate effectively. This creates a higher risk of insider trading, where individuals with access to privileged information can exploit it for personal gain. Insider trading undermines the fairness and integrity of the market, as it allows certain individuals to profit at the expense of other investors. The absence of strict regulations and oversight mechanisms can make it difficult to detect and prevent insider trading activities in the cryptocurrency market.
5. Lack of Transparency: Transparency is a vital component of efficient and fair markets. In the cryptocurrency market,

however, the level of transparency can vary significantly. While blockchain technology offers transparency at the transactional level, certain aspects such as ownership identities, trading volumes, and market activities may lack transparency. This opacity can make it challenging for investors to assess the true liquidity, market depth, and overall health of the cryptocurrency market. The lack of transparency can create an environment prone to market manipulation and hinder the ability of investors to make informed decisions.

6. Legal and Regulatory Risks: Investing in cryptocurrencies can also expose investors to legal and regulatory risks. The evolving nature of regulations and the differing approaches of governments and regulatory bodies worldwide can result in legal uncertainties. Cryptocurrency investments may be subject to changes in tax regulations, restrictions on usage or ownership, and even outright bans in some jurisdictions. These legal and regulatory risks can impact the value and viability of cryptocurrencies, potentially leading to significant losses for investors.

It is crucial for investors to be aware of the lack of regulations and the risks associated with market manipulation when considering investments in cryptocurrencies. Conducting thorough research, staying informed about regulatory developments, and exercising caution when selecting cryptocurrency platforms and service providers can help mitigate some of these risks.

4.1.3 Potential for Fraud and Security Risks

Alongside price fluctuations, market manipulation, and regulatory challenges, investing in cryptocurrencies also carries the risk of fraud and security breaches. In this subsection, we will delve into the potential for fraud and security risks in the cryptocurrency market.

1. Scams and Ponzi Schemes: The decentralized and less regulated nature of the cryptocurrency market makes it an attractive breeding ground for scams and Ponzi schemes. Unscrupulous individuals or organizations may create fraudulent cryptocurrencies, promising high returns or exclusive investment opportunities. Investors must exercise caution and conduct thorough due diligence to avoid falling victim to these scams. It is crucial to verify the legitimacy of the projects, assess the credibility of the teams behind them, and be wary of promises that sound too good to be true.
2. Hacking and Cybersecurity Risks: Cryptocurrencies rely on digital wallets and exchanges for storage and trading. However, these digital assets are susceptible to hacking and cybersecurity risks. Hackers can target exchanges or individuals' wallets, attempting to steal funds. The security breaches of prominent exchanges in the past serve as a reminder of the vulnerabilities in the cryptocurrency ecosystem. Investors must take precautions to secure their wallets and choose reputable and secure platforms for trading and storage. Implementing strong security measures, such as using hardware wallets and enabling two-factor authentication, can help mitigate the risk of theft or unauthorized access.
3. Phishing and Social Engineering Attacks: Phishing attacks are prevalent in the cryptocurrency space. Scammers may attempt to deceive users into revealing their private keys, passwords, or other sensitive information through fake websites or emails. Social engineering tactics are employed to manipulate individuals into providing access to their

cryptocurrency holdings. Investors should exercise caution and be vigilant about protecting their personal information. It is important to verify the authenticity of websites, use secure communication channels, and refrain from sharing sensitive information with unknown or unverified sources.

4. Irreversible Transactions: Cryptocurrency transactions, once confirmed on the blockchain, are typically irreversible. While this immutability ensures the integrity of the blockchain, it also means that if funds are sent to the wrong address or if a transaction is conducted with fraudulent parties, it may be challenging or impossible to recover the funds. Investors must exercise caution when entering wallet addresses or conducting transactions, double-checking the recipient's address to avoid irreversible mistakes.
5. Lack of Consumer Protections: Cryptocurrency investments may not have the same level of consumer protections as traditional financial assets. Unlike bank accounts or brokerage accounts, which may be insured by governmental agencies, cryptocurrencies held in digital wallets are not protected in the same manner. If an individual loses access to their wallet or falls victim to theft or fraud, recovery options may be limited or non-existent. Investors must take responsibility for their own security measures and be aware of the potential lack of recourse in case of loss or theft.
6. Initial Coin Offering (ICO) Risks: ICOs, which are fundraising events where new cryptocurrencies are issued to investors, have been associated with various risks. Some ICOs may be fraudulent or fail to deliver on their promises. Investors may also face challenges with liquidity and market acceptance once the ICO concludes. Thorough due diligence is crucial before participating in an ICO, including reviewing the project's whitepaper, understanding the team's

background, and assessing the viability and potential risks associated with the offering.

It is important for investors to be aware of the potential for fraud and security risks in the cryptocurrency market. By staying informed, conducting thorough research, implementing robust security measures, and exercising caution when interacting with the cryptocurrency ecosystem, investors can minimize the likelihood of falling victim to fraud or security breaches.

4.2 Lack of Intrinsic Value and Fundamental Analysis

In addition to the volatility, regulatory challenges, and security risks discussed earlier, investing in cryptocurrencies poses concerns related to the lack of intrinsic value and the limitations of fundamental analysis. In this subsection, we will explore these cons in more detail.

1. Lack of Intrinsic Value: Unlike traditional assets such as stocks or real estate, cryptocurrencies often lack tangible assets or cash flows that can be used to determine their intrinsic value. The value of cryptocurrencies is primarily driven by market demand, speculation, and investor sentiment. While blockchain technology and the potential utility of specific cryptocurrencies can contribute to their perceived value, the absence of underlying physical assets or cash flow-generating activities makes it challenging to assess their intrinsic worth. This lack of intrinsic value can make it difficult for investors to determine whether the current market prices are justified or if they are purely driven by speculative forces.
2. Limited Fundamental Analysis: Fundamental analysis, which involves evaluating the financial health, business model, and growth prospects of an asset, is a common approach in

traditional investing. However, cryptocurrencies present challenges when applying fundamental analysis techniques. The traditional metrics used in fundamental analysis, such as earnings, revenue, and cash flow, may not be readily applicable to cryptocurrencies. Instead, investors often rely on alternative metrics like transaction volume, network activity, and community adoption to assess the potential value and growth prospects of cryptocurrencies. However, these metrics may have limitations and may not provide a comprehensive understanding of a cryptocurrency's long-term viability.

3. Market Irrationality: The cryptocurrency market is known for its speculative nature and high levels of market irrationality. Prices can be driven by hype, social media trends, or speculative buying and selling, rather than rational valuation based on fundamental factors. This market irrationality can lead to significant price bubbles or crashes that are disconnected from the underlying value of cryptocurrencies. Investors who rely solely on fundamental analysis may find it challenging to navigate this volatile and irrational market environment.
4. Lack of Financial Disclosures: In traditional financial markets, companies are required to provide regular financial disclosures and reports that aid in fundamental analysis. However, cryptocurrencies and blockchain projects often operate in a decentralized manner without centralized reporting requirements. This lack of standardized financial disclosures makes it challenging for investors to obtain reliable and comprehensive information about the financial health and performance of specific cryptocurrencies or blockchain projects. As a result, assessing the fundamental strength or weaknesses of cryptocurrencies can be more

challenging compared to traditional assets.

5. Influence of Market Sentiment: The cryptocurrency market is highly influenced by market sentiment and investor psychology. Positive or negative news, regulatory developments, or market trends can significantly impact the prices of cryptocurrencies, even without any substantial changes in their underlying fundamentals. This market sentiment-driven volatility can make it challenging for investors to rely solely on fundamental analysis when making investment decisions.

It is important for investors to recognize the limitations of fundamental analysis in the cryptocurrency market. While fundamental factors may still provide some insights, investors should also consider other factors such as technological innovation, adoption trends, and market sentiment when evaluating potential cryptocurrency investments.

4.2.1 Assessing the True Value of Cryptocurrencies

When it comes to investing in cryptocurrencies, one of the significant challenges is assessing their true value. Unlike traditional assets with established valuation models, cryptocurrencies present unique complexities. In this subsection, we will explore the difficulties associated with determining the true value of cryptocurrencies.

1. Lack of Established Valuation Models: Cryptocurrencies are relatively new assets, and as such, there are no well-established valuation models comparable to those used for stocks or bonds. Traditional valuation methods, such as discounted cash flow analysis or price-to-earnings ratios, may not be directly applicable to cryptocurrencies. The lack of cash flows, earnings, or dividends associated with

cryptocurrencies makes it challenging to determine their fair value based on traditional financial metrics.

2. Reliance on Market Demand and Sentiment: The value of cryptocurrencies is primarily driven by market demand and investor sentiment. Factors such as adoption rates, network activity, and investor perception influence the market prices of cryptocurrencies. However, these factors can be highly subjective and prone to rapid changes. The reliance on market sentiment introduces a level of uncertainty and volatility that can make it difficult to assess the true underlying value of cryptocurrencies.
3. Utility and Network Effects: The utility and network effects of a cryptocurrency play a significant role in determining its value. Utility refers to the practical usefulness of a cryptocurrency within a specific ecosystem or for a particular purpose. Network effects occur when the value of a cryptocurrency increases as more individuals or entities adopt and use it. Evaluating the potential utility and network effects of a cryptocurrency requires a deep understanding of the underlying technology, its potential applications, and the competitive landscape. This analysis can be complex and subjective, adding to the challenges of assessing the true value of cryptocurrencies.
4. Speculation and Market Manipulation: The cryptocurrency market is known for its speculative nature, driven by short-term price fluctuations and market manipulation. Speculative buying and selling can lead to price bubbles or crashes that may not align with the fundamental value of a cryptocurrency. Market manipulation practices, such as pump-and-dump schemes or coordinated trading activities, can distort market prices and make it even more challenging to assess the true value of cryptocurrencies.

5. Lack of Comparable Assets: In traditional financial markets, investors often compare assets within the same industry or sector to evaluate their relative value. However, cryptocurrencies are unique digital assets with varying characteristics, use cases, and technological underpinnings. This lack of directly comparable assets makes it challenging to benchmark or establish a valuation framework for cryptocurrencies.

To overcome these challenges, investors may employ alternative valuation approaches specific to cryptocurrencies. These may include metrics such as on-chain analysis, transaction volume, user adoption, developer activity, and token economics. However, it's important to note that these methods also have their limitations and may not provide a definitive measure of a cryptocurrency's true value.

When investing in cryptocurrencies, it is essential for investors to recognize the complexities involved in assessing their true value. Conducting thorough research, understanding the underlying technology and ecosystem, and considering multiple factors beyond traditional financial metrics can help investors make more informed decisions.

4.2.2 Evaluating Investment Opportunities in the Absence of Traditional Valuation Metrics

Investing in cryptocurrencies poses a unique challenge when it comes to evaluating investment opportunities. In the absence of traditional valuation metrics, investors need to adopt alternative approaches to assess the potential of cryptocurrencies. In this subsection, we will explore some strategies for evaluating investment opportunities in the cryptocurrency market.

1. Technological Analysis: One approach to evaluating

cryptocurrencies is through technological analysis. This involves assessing the underlying technology, such as the blockchain protocol, consensus mechanism, scalability, and security features. Understanding the technological advancements and innovations within a cryptocurrency project can provide insights into its potential for adoption and long-term viability. Evaluating factors like developer community activity, codebase quality, and upgrades can help investors gauge the strength of a cryptocurrency's technology.

2. Team and Community: The team behind a cryptocurrency project plays a crucial role in its success. Evaluating the expertise, experience, and track record of the development team and advisors can provide insights into the project's potential. Additionally, assessing the size and engagement of the community surrounding a cryptocurrency project can indicate its level of support and adoption. Active communities, developer participation, and partnerships can contribute to the project's growth and increase its potential value.
3. Use Case and Adoption: Examining the use case and potential adoption of a cryptocurrency is another important factor to consider. Assessing whether a cryptocurrency solves a real-world problem or offers a unique value proposition can help determine its potential market demand. Analyzing factors such as partnerships, collaborations, and pilot programs that showcase real-world adoption can provide insights into the growth prospects of a cryptocurrency.
4. Market and Competitive Analysis: Understanding the market dynamics and competitive landscape is crucial when evaluating investment opportunities in cryptocurrencies. Analyzing factors such as market size, potential competition, regulatory environment, and barriers to entry can help

investors assess the potential growth and sustainability of a cryptocurrency project. Market analysis involves researching trends, industry developments, and market sentiment to gauge the potential demand for a particular cryptocurrency.

5. Risk Assessment: Investing in cryptocurrencies inherently carries risks, and assessing these risks is essential for making informed investment decisions. Evaluating factors such as regulatory risks, market volatility, technological vulnerabilities, and project-specific risks can help investors understand the potential downsides associated with a cryptocurrency investment. Conducting thorough due diligence and risk assessment can help mitigate potential losses and protect investors' capital.

While traditional valuation metrics may not be directly applicable to cryptocurrencies, adopting a comprehensive approach that combines technological analysis, team evaluation, market analysis, and risk assessment can provide a framework for evaluating investment opportunities in the cryptocurrency market. However, it is important to note that investing in cryptocurrencies still carries inherent risks, and investors should carefully consider their risk tolerance and seek professional advice when necessary.

4.3 Regulatory and Legal Challenges

Investing in cryptocurrencies comes with regulatory and legal challenges that investors need to consider. In this section, we will explore the potential drawbacks and risks associated with the regulatory and legal landscape of cryptocurrencies.

1. Lack of Regulatory Clarity: Cryptocurrencies operate in a relatively nascent and rapidly evolving regulatory environment. The lack of clear and consistent regulations

across different jurisdictions can create uncertainty and challenges for investors. Regulatory frameworks for cryptocurrencies vary widely, ranging from outright bans in some countries to more accommodating or supportive regulations in others. The absence of unified regulations can lead to confusion, making it difficult for investors to navigate the legal landscape and assess the long-term viability of their investments.

2. Regulatory Changes: Regulatory frameworks surrounding cryptocurrencies are subject to frequent changes. Governments and regulatory authorities may introduce new laws or policies that impact the use, trading, or taxation of cryptocurrencies. Such changes can have a significant impact on the value and market sentiment of cryptocurrencies. Investors need to stay informed about regulatory developments and adapt their investment strategies accordingly.
3. Security and Consumer Protection: Cryptocurrencies are susceptible to security breaches, hacking, and fraud. While blockchain technology itself provides security features, vulnerabilities can still exist in exchanges, wallets, and other related infrastructure. The decentralized nature of cryptocurrencies makes it challenging to retrieve lost or stolen funds. Additionally, the lack of consumer protection mechanisms and the irreversible nature of cryptocurrency transactions can leave investors vulnerable to scams and fraudulent activities.
4. Anti-Money Laundering (AML) and Know Your Customer (KYC) Compliance: Cryptocurrencies have attracted attention from regulators due to their potential misuse in illicit activities, such as money laundering and terrorism financing. As a result, regulatory authorities have introduced

AML and KYC requirements for cryptocurrency exchanges and service providers. These regulations aim to enhance transparency and combat illicit activities but may add operational and compliance burdens for investors and service providers.

5. Taxation: Tax regulations regarding cryptocurrencies vary across jurisdictions. Investors are often required to report their cryptocurrency holdings, transactions, and capital gains for tax purposes. However, determining the appropriate tax treatment and complying with reporting obligations can be complex, especially considering the decentralized nature of cryptocurrencies and the lack of standardized reporting mechanisms. Failure to comply with tax regulations can result in penalties and legal consequences.
6. Legal and Regulatory Risks for Initial Coin Offerings (ICOs): ICOs, a fundraising method utilized by cryptocurrency projects, have faced scrutiny from regulatory authorities. The legal status of ICOs and the tokens issued through them can vary, and regulatory authorities may consider certain ICOs as securities offerings, subject to securities regulations. Investors need to be aware of the legal and regulatory risks associated with participating in ICOs and ensure compliance with applicable regulations.

Navigating the regulatory and legal challenges associated with cryptocurrencies requires a thorough understanding of the regulatory environment in relevant jurisdictions and compliance with applicable laws. It is important for investors to stay updated on regulatory developments, engage with reputable exchanges and service providers, and seek professional advice when necessary.

4.3.1 Government Regulations and Potential Bans

Government regulations and the potential for cryptocurrency bans pose significant challenges and risks to investors. In this subsection, we will delve into the regulatory landscape and the possibility of cryptocurrency bans.

1. Regulatory Uncertainty: Cryptocurrencies operate in a regulatory landscape that is constantly evolving. Governments around the world are grappling with how to regulate cryptocurrencies due to their unique characteristics and potential impact on financial systems. The lack of clear and consistent regulations can create uncertainty for investors, as they may be unsure about the legality and regulatory implications of their cryptocurrency investments.
2. Increased Regulatory Scrutiny: Cryptocurrencies have attracted increased regulatory scrutiny due to concerns such as money laundering, tax evasion, and investor protection. Regulatory authorities may impose stricter regulations on cryptocurrency exchanges, initial coin offerings (ICOs), and other aspects of the cryptocurrency ecosystem. Compliance with these regulations may involve additional costs and operational burdens for cryptocurrency market participants.
3. Possibility of Bans: Some governments have taken a more hostile approach towards cryptocurrencies and have either imposed strict regulations or outright banned their use. Bans can restrict or prohibit the trading, mining, or possession of cryptocurrencies within a particular jurisdiction. These bans can have a significant impact on the value and liquidity of cryptocurrencies, making it difficult for investors to trade or exit their positions.
4. Impact on Market Sentiment: Government actions, such as regulatory crackdowns or the announcement of potential bans, can create negative market sentiment towards

cryptocurrencies. Fears of stricter regulations or bans can lead to increased selling pressure and price volatility. The uncertainty surrounding the regulatory environment can deter institutional investors and mainstream adoption, potentially impeding the growth of the cryptocurrency market.

5. International Regulatory Disparities: Cryptocurrency regulations vary widely across different countries and jurisdictions. While some countries have embraced cryptocurrencies and implemented favorable regulations, others have taken a more cautious or hostile approach. This disparity can create challenges for investors operating across multiple jurisdictions and can impact the global liquidity and accessibility of cryptocurrencies.
6. Regulatory Compliance and KYC/AML Requirements: Regulatory compliance measures, such as Know Your Customer (KYC) and Anti-Money Laundering (AML) requirements, can add complexities for investors. Exchanges and service providers may require thorough identity verification processes and transaction monitoring to ensure compliance with regulations. These requirements may impede the privacy and anonymity that some investors seek from cryptocurrencies.

It is crucial for investors to stay informed about the regulatory landscape in their respective jurisdictions and the potential risks associated with government regulations and bans. Assessing the regulatory climate, engaging with compliant service providers, and understanding the legal implications of investing in cryptocurrencies can help investors navigate these challenges.

4.3.2 Taxation and Reporting Requirements

Taxation and reporting requirements are important considerations for investors in cryptocurrencies. In this subsection, we will explore the challenges and obligations related to taxation and reporting in the cryptocurrency market.

1. Complex Tax Regulations: Tax regulations surrounding cryptocurrencies can be complex and vary significantly across jurisdictions. Determining the tax treatment of cryptocurrencies, including capital gains, income tax, and reporting obligations, can be challenging. The lack of standardized guidelines and the evolving nature of the cryptocurrency market make it difficult for investors to navigate the tax landscape effectively.
2. Reporting Cryptocurrency Transactions: Many tax authorities require individuals to report their cryptocurrency transactions, including purchases, sales, and conversions. This can involve tracking and reporting a large volume of transactions, which can be time-consuming and burdensome for investors. Failure to report cryptocurrency transactions accurately and timely can result in penalties and legal consequences.
3. Valuation Challenges: Valuing cryptocurrencies for tax purposes can be challenging due to their price volatility and the lack of consistent valuation methods. Tax authorities may require investors to determine the fair market value of their cryptocurrency holdings at the time of each transaction or at the end of the tax year. This can be particularly difficult when converting between different cryptocurrencies or when cryptocurrencies are used in decentralized finance (DeFi) protocols.
4. Airdrops, Forks, and Token Swaps: Certain events in the cryptocurrency space, such as airdrops (free distribution of

tokens), forks (creation of a new cryptocurrency from an existing one), and token swaps (migration to a new blockchain or protocol), can have tax implications. Investors may be required to report and potentially pay taxes on the received tokens or the resulting gains or losses from these events.

5. International Tax Considerations: For investors operating across international borders, additional complexities arise due to different tax laws and reporting requirements in each jurisdiction. Transactions involving cryptocurrency exchanges, foreign investments, or cross-border transfers may trigger tax obligations in multiple countries, requiring investors to navigate complex international tax regulations.
6. Regulatory Scrutiny and Tax Enforcement: As governments and tax authorities become more aware of the cryptocurrency market, they are increasing their efforts to enforce tax compliance. Cryptocurrency exchanges and service providers are increasingly subject to reporting requirements and may be compelled to disclose customer information to tax authorities. This raises concerns about the privacy and anonymity associated with cryptocurrencies.

To ensure compliance with tax regulations and reporting requirements, investors should consult with tax professionals who are knowledgeable about cryptocurrency taxation. Keeping accurate records of transactions, seeking guidance on proper valuation methods, and staying updated on changes in tax regulations can help investors fulfill their tax obligations and mitigate the risks associated with non-compliance.

Chapter 5: Investment Strategies for Cryptocurrencies

5.1 Long-term vs. Short-term Investment Approaches

When investing in cryptocurrencies, investors have the option to adopt different investment strategies based on their goals, risk tolerance, and time horizons. In this chapter, we will explore two primary approaches: long-term and short-term investment strategies.

5.1.1 Long-term Investment Approach

The long-term investment approach involves holding cryptocurrencies for an extended period, typically years, with the expectation of capital appreciation over time. Here are some key characteristics and considerations of a long-term investment approach:

1. Fundamental Analysis: Long-term investors focus on the underlying fundamentals of a cryptocurrency, such as its technology, adoption potential, use case, and team. They evaluate the long-term viability and growth prospects of the project before making an investment.
2. HODLing: HODL (Hold On for Dear Life) is a term often used in the cryptocurrency community to describe the strategy of holding onto cryptocurrencies despite short-term price fluctuations. Long-term investors believe in the long-term potential of the technology and aim to benefit from the growth of the cryptocurrency ecosystem over time.
3. Dollar-Cost Averaging: Long-term investors often employ a strategy called dollar-cost averaging, where they invest a fixed amount of money at regular intervals, regardless of the current price of the cryptocurrency. This strategy reduces the impact of short-term price volatility and allows investors to

accumulate cryptocurrencies over time.

4. Patience and Conviction: Long-term investors understand that the cryptocurrency market can be highly volatile in the short term. They have the patience to weather market fluctuations and maintain conviction in their investment thesis, believing that the technology and market will mature over time.
5. Tax Efficiency: Long-term investments may qualify for favorable tax treatment in some jurisdictions. Holding cryptocurrencies for a specified period may result in lower tax rates on capital gains compared to short-term trading.

5.1.2 Short-term Investment Approach

The short-term investment approach involves actively trading cryptocurrencies to take advantage of short-term price movements and generate profits. Here are some key characteristics and considerations of a short-term investment approach:

1. Technical Analysis: Short-term traders rely heavily on technical analysis, studying price charts, patterns, and market indicators to identify short-term trading opportunities. They aim to exploit short-term price fluctuations and trends for potential profit.
2. Active Trading: Short-term traders engage in frequent buying and selling of cryptocurrencies to capitalize on short-term price movements. They may employ various trading strategies, such as scalping, day trading, or swing trading, depending on their preferred timeframes.
3. Risk Management: Short-term trading involves higher risks due to the volatile nature of the cryptocurrency market. Traders implement risk management strategies, such as setting stop-loss orders, managing position sizes, and

diversifying their trading portfolio, to protect against potential losses.

4. Market News and Sentiment: Short-term traders closely follow market news, announcements, and sentiment to gauge potential market movements. They aim to react quickly to market events and capitalize on price fluctuations driven by news and market sentiment.
5. Tax Implications: Short-term trading may result in more frequent taxable events, as each trade can trigger a taxable event, potentially leading to complex tax reporting and higher tax liabilities compared to long-term investments.

It is important for investors to align their investment strategy with their goals, risk tolerance, and time horizon. Long-term investments require patience, conviction, and a focus on fundamentals, while short-term trading demands active monitoring, technical analysis skills, and risk management. Investors should carefully consider their personal circumstances and seek professional advice before adopting any investment strategy.

5.2 Dollar-Cost Averaging

Dollar-cost averaging is an investment strategy that involves investing a fixed amount of money at regular intervals, regardless of the price of the cryptocurrency. This strategy aims to reduce the impact of short-term price volatility and allows investors to accumulate cryptocurrencies over time. Here are the key aspects and benefits of dollar-cost averaging:

1. Regular Investments: With dollar-cost averaging, investors commit to investing a fixed amount of money at predefined intervals, such as weekly, monthly, or quarterly. Regardless of whether the price of the cryptocurrency is high or low at the

time of investment, the same fixed amount is invested consistently.

2. Smoothing Out Market Fluctuations: By investing at regular intervals, dollar-cost averaging helps to smooth out the impact of market fluctuations. When prices are high, the fixed investment amount buys fewer units of the cryptocurrency, and when prices are low, the fixed investment amount buys more units. This approach can mitigate the risk of making large investments at unfavorable prices.
3. Potential Lower Average Cost: Dollar-cost averaging allows investors to buy more units when prices are low and fewer units when prices are high. Over time, this strategy can potentially result in a lower average cost per unit compared to making a lump-sum investment. It takes advantage of the natural volatility in the cryptocurrency market by accumulating more units during periods of price decline.
4. Emotional Discipline: Dollar-cost averaging helps investors to maintain a disciplined approach and avoid making impulsive investment decisions based on short-term price movements or market sentiment. By adhering to a predetermined investment plan, investors can stay focused on their long-term investment goals and avoid succumbing to emotional biases.
5. Mitigating Timing Risk: Trying to time the market and make investments at the most opportune moments is challenging, even for experienced investors. Dollar-cost averaging reduces the risk of mistiming the market by spreading investments over a longer period. This strategy allows investors to participate in the potential long-term growth of cryptocurrencies, regardless of short-term market fluctuations.
6. Lower Entry Barrier: Dollar-cost averaging enables investors

to enter the cryptocurrency market gradually, starting with smaller investment amounts. This can be advantageous for investors who may not have a large amount of capital to invest upfront but still want to participate in the potential returns of cryptocurrencies.

While dollar-cost averaging can be an effective investment strategy, it is important to note that it does not guarantee profits or protection against losses. The cryptocurrency market remains volatile, and prices can fluctuate significantly. Investors should carefully consider their risk tolerance, financial goals, and consult with professionals when designing an investment plan.

5.3 Fundamental Analysis and Researching Projects

Fundamental analysis is an investment approach that involves evaluating the underlying factors and intrinsic value of a cryptocurrency project to assess its potential for long-term growth and success. Conducting thorough research on projects is essential for making informed investment decisions. Here are the key aspects and benefits of fundamental analysis and researching projects:

1. Understanding the Technology: Fundamental analysis begins with understanding the technology behind a cryptocurrency project. Investors delve into the whitepapers, technical documentation, and codebase to assess the innovation, scalability, security, and practical applications of the technology. This understanding helps investors gauge the long-term viability and potential adoption of the project.
2. Evaluating the Team and Community: Assessing the team behind a cryptocurrency project is crucial. Investors examine the expertise, experience, and track record of the core team members, as well as their commitment and vision for the

project. Additionally, analyzing the community surrounding the project, including developers, contributors, and users, provides insights into the level of support and engagement it receives.

3. Market Opportunity and Competition: Fundamental analysis involves evaluating the market opportunity and potential demand for the cryptocurrency project. Investors assess factors such as the size of the target market, competition from existing projects, and the project's unique value proposition. Understanding the competitive landscape helps investors gauge the project's ability to gain market share and sustain growth.
4. Token Economics and Utility: Fundamental analysis includes examining the token economics and utility of the cryptocurrency. Investors assess factors such as the token's use cases within the project ecosystem, its distribution model, and any economic incentives provided to token holders. Analyzing the tokenomics helps investors understand the potential value and demand dynamics of the cryptocurrency.
5. Partnerships and Adoption: Researching the partnerships and collaborations of a cryptocurrency project provides insights into its potential for real-world adoption. Investors look for partnerships with established companies, academic institutions, or industry leaders that can contribute to the project's growth and adoption. The level of integration and acceptance of the project within relevant industries and ecosystems is a crucial factor to consider.
6. Financial and Governance Transparency: Fundamental analysis involves assessing the financial health and governance practices of the project. Investors analyze financial reports, funding sources, and token allocation to understand the project's financial stability and transparency. Furthermore,

evaluating the project's governance model and decision-making processes helps investors gauge its ability to adapt and evolve over time.

By conducting comprehensive fundamental analysis and researching projects, investors can make informed investment decisions based on a thorough understanding of the cryptocurrency's technology, market potential, team, community, and financial aspects. It allows investors to identify projects with solid foundations and growth potential, reducing the risk of investing in projects with questionable fundamentals.

Chapter 6: Evaluating Cryptocurrency Projects

6.1 Understanding Whitepapers and Project Goals

Whitepapers play a crucial role in understanding the goals, technology, and potential of a cryptocurrency project. They provide detailed information about the project's vision, technical specifications, and implementation plans. Evaluating whitepapers is essential for assessing the viability and potential of a cryptocurrency project. In this chapter, we will explore the importance of understanding whitepapers and project goals when evaluating cryptocurrency projects.

6.1.1 Importance of Whitepapers:

Whitepapers serve as the foundational documents for cryptocurrency projects. They outline the project's objectives, technology, and roadmap, providing insights into the project's purpose, functionality, and potential impact. Here are key aspects to consider when evaluating whitepapers:

1. Vision and Goals: Whitepapers define the project's vision and goals, explaining the problem the project aims to solve or the innovation it aims to introduce. Understanding the project's purpose and objectives is essential for assessing its potential value and alignment with your investment goals.
2. Technology and Architecture: Whitepapers provide technical details about the underlying technology and architecture of the cryptocurrency project. They explain the consensus mechanism, data structures, cryptography, and other technical aspects. Evaluating the technology helps determine the project's scalability, security, and feasibility.
3. Use Cases and Applications: Whitepapers describe the use

cases and potential applications of the cryptocurrency project. They highlight how the technology can be utilized and the value it can bring to various industries or sectors. Assessing the project's use cases helps gauge its potential for adoption and market demand.

4. Roadmap and Milestones: Whitepapers often include a roadmap that outlines the project's development and implementation plan. The roadmap provides a timeline of key milestones, including the project's launch, major updates, partnerships, and integration with external platforms. Evaluating the roadmap helps assess the project's progress and its ability to deliver on its promises.
5. Tokenomics and Distribution: Whitepapers provide information about the project's tokenomics, including details about the token supply, distribution, and utility. Understanding the token economics helps evaluate the project's economic model, incentives for token holders, and potential value appreciation.
6. Team and Advisors: Whitepapers often introduce the project's team members and advisors. Assessing the team's expertise, experience, and credibility can provide insights into the project's potential for success. Additionally, evaluating the background and industry connections of the project's advisors can add further credibility to the project.

6.1.2 Evaluating Project Goals:

In addition to understanding whitepapers, evaluating the project's goals is crucial for assessing its potential. Consider the following factors when evaluating the goals of a cryptocurrency project:

1. Market Demand: Assess the market demand for the project's proposed solution or innovation. Research the existing

market landscape and determine if there is a genuine need for the project's offering.

2. Competitive Advantage: Evaluate the project's competitive advantage and differentiation. Understand how it stands out from existing projects in terms of technology, features, partnerships, or market positioning.
3. Adoption Potential: Analyze the project's potential for adoption and its ability to gain a user base. Consider factors such as partnerships, marketing strategies, target audience, and the project's plan for user acquisition and retention.
4. Execution and Roadmap: Evaluate the project's execution capabilities by examining its progress, achievements, and adherence to the stated roadmap. Look for evidence of successful milestones and delivery on promises.
5. Community Engagement: Assess the project's community engagement and support. Evaluate the size, activity, and sentiment of the community surrounding the project. A vibrant and supportive community can contribute to the project's long-term success.

Understanding whitepapers and project goals provides a solid foundation for evaluating cryptocurrency projects. It allows investors to assess the project's purpose, technology, roadmap, and potential for success. By conducting thorough evaluations, investors can make informed decisions and select projects that align with their investment strategies and risk tolerance.

6.2 Assessing Team Expertise and Credibility

The expertise and credibility of the team behind a cryptocurrency project are critical factors to consider when evaluating its potential for success. A strong and capable team increases the likelihood of effective project execution and the ability to overcome challenges. In this section, we will explore the importance of assessing team expertise and credibility when evaluating cryptocurrency projects.

6.2.1 Evaluating Team Expertise:

1. Core Team Members: Assess the qualifications, experience, and track record of the project's core team members. Look for team members with relevant expertise in areas such as blockchain technology, finance, software development, and business development. Consider their previous experience in successfully executing similar projects or their involvement in reputable organizations.
2. Technical Competence: Evaluate the technical competence of the team members responsible for developing the project's technology. Consider their proficiency in blockchain development, smart contract programming, and other relevant technical skills. Look for evidence of their contributions to the open-source community, participation in relevant conferences, or publications in respected journals.
3. Advisory Board: Examine the composition and credibility of the project's advisory board. Advisors with notable industry experience, academic background, or influential connections can add significant value to the project. Research the advisors' involvement in other successful projects and their expertise in relevant domains.
4. Team Cohesion and Collaboration: Assess the cohesion and collaboration within the team. Look for evidence of effective communication, shared vision, and a collaborative work environment. A cohesive team is more likely to work efficiently, make sound decisions, and overcome challenges together.

6.2.2 Evaluating Team Credibility:

1. Transparency and Communication: Evaluate the team's transparency and communication with the community. Look for regular updates, responsiveness to inquiries, and clarity in conveying project progress, achievements, and challenges. Transparency builds trust and demonstrates the team's commitment to keeping stakeholders informed.
2. Reputation and Integrity: Research the team's reputation and integrity within the cryptocurrency community. Look for any past controversies, scams, or unethical practices associated with team members. A team with a history of questionable conduct or negative reputation may raise concerns about the project's credibility.
3. Previous Successes and Failures: Consider the team's track record, including both successes and failures. Examine their previous projects, whether in the cryptocurrency space or other relevant industries. Look for indications of resilience, adaptability, and the ability to learn from past experiences.
4. Network and Connections: Assess the team's network and connections within the cryptocurrency industry and other relevant sectors. Strong connections can provide access to resources, partnerships, and valuable insights. Consider the team's ability to leverage their network to support the project's growth and adoption.
5. Commitment and Vision: Evaluate the team's commitment to the project and their long-term vision. Look for indications of dedication, passion, and alignment with the project's goals. A team that is genuinely committed to the project is more likely to persevere through challenges and work towards its success.

By thoroughly evaluating team expertise and credibility, investors can gain confidence in the project's ability to deliver on its promises and navigate the dynamic cryptocurrency landscape. However, it's important to note that team assessment is just one aspect of a comprehensive evaluation process. It should be combined with other factors such as technology, market demand, and project viability to make well-informed investment decisions.

6.3 Analyzing Market Adoption and Competition

Analyzing market adoption and competition is a crucial step in evaluating the potential of a cryptocurrency project. Understanding the current state of adoption and the competitive landscape provides insights into the project's viability, growth potential, and market positioning. In this section, we will explore the importance of analyzing market adoption and competition when evaluating cryptocurrency projects.

6.3.1 Market Adoption Analysis:

1. User Base and Growth: Evaluate the size and growth rate of the project's user base. Look for indications of increasing adoption and active engagement from users. Consider metrics such as the number of active wallets, daily transactions, and community participation. A growing user base suggests increasing acceptance and demand for the project.
2. Real-World Use Cases: Assess the project's real-world use cases and its potential for practical application. Investigate whether the project addresses a genuine problem or offers a unique value proposition. Look for partnerships or collaborations with established businesses or organizations that can drive adoption. Projects with tangible use cases are more likely to gain traction and see widespread adoption.
3. Developer Community: Examine the size and activity of the project's developer community. A vibrant developer

community indicates a strong ecosystem around the project, fostering innovation, and providing technical support. Active developer engagement is essential for the continuous improvement and evolution of the project.

4. Geographic Reach: Consider the geographic reach of the project's adoption. Evaluate whether the project has gained traction in specific regions or markets. Understanding the project's global reach helps assess its potential for scalability and expansion.

6.3.2 Competition Analysis:

1. Market Share and Positioning: Analyze the project's market share and its positioning compared to competitors. Evaluate factors such as technology, user adoption, partnerships, and market capitalization. Consider how the project differentiates itself and its potential for gaining a larger market share in the future.
2. Competitor Analysis: Conduct a comprehensive analysis of the project's competitors. Assess their strengths, weaknesses, and market presence. Identify projects that have similar offerings or target the same market segment. Understanding the competitive landscape helps determine the project's unique value proposition and its ability to differentiate itself from others.
3. Partnerships and Integrations: Evaluate the partnerships and integrations the project has established. Look for collaborations with established industry players, influential organizations, or blockchain interoperability initiatives. Strong partnerships can provide a competitive advantage and increase the project's chances of success.
4. Barriers to Entry: Consider the barriers to entry in the project's market segment. Evaluate the challenges new

competitors would face in entering the market and gaining adoption. Projects that have established a strong presence and built significant network effects may have a higher barrier to entry, giving them a competitive advantage.

5. Innovation and Roadmap: Assess the project's innovation capabilities and its ability to stay ahead of the competition. Evaluate the project's roadmap, upcoming features, and planned updates. Look for indications of ongoing development and a commitment to continuous improvement.

By conducting a thorough analysis of market adoption and competition, investors can gain insights into the project's growth potential, competitive advantage, and market positioning. This analysis helps in understanding the project's ability to gain market share, overcome competition, and sustain long-term growth.

Chapter 7: Wallets and Security Measures

7.1 Different Types of Cryptocurrency Wallets

Cryptocurrency wallets are essential tools for securely storing and managing digital assets. They provide a secure way to store private keys, enabling users to access and transact with their cryptocurrencies. In this chapter, we will explore the different types of cryptocurrency wallets available and their unique characteristics.

7.1.1 Hardware Wallets:

Hardware wallets are physical devices designed specifically for storing cryptocurrencies securely. They are offline, cold storage wallets that provide an extra layer of protection against online threats. Hardware wallets generate and store private keys offline, making them less susceptible to hacking attempts. Users can connect the hardware wallet to a computer or mobile device when they need to sign transactions. Examples of popular hardware wallets include Ledger, Trezor, and KeepKey.

Advantages:

- Enhanced security: Private keys are stored offline, reducing the risk of hacking.
- User-friendly: Hardware wallets often have intuitive interfaces, making them easy to use.
- Multi-currency support: Many hardware wallets support a wide range of cryptocurrencies.
- Backup and recovery: Hardware wallets offer backup and recovery options in case the device is lost or damaged.

Disadvantages:

- Cost: Hardware wallets are generally more expensive than other types of wallets.
- Accessibility: Users need to have the physical device with them to access their funds, which may not be convenient for frequent transactions.

7.1.2 Software Wallets:

Software wallets are applications or software programs that can be installed on computers, smartphones, or tablets. They allow users to manage their cryptocurrencies through an interface provided by the wallet provider. Software wallets can be further categorized into two types:

7.1.2.1 Desktop Wallets:

Desktop wallets are installed and run on personal computers or laptops. They offer a higher level of security compared to online wallets as they are not constantly connected to the internet. Desktop wallets store private keys locally, giving users full control over their funds. Some popular desktop wallets include Exodus, Electrum, and Atomic Wallet.

Advantages:

- Enhanced security: Private keys are stored locally, reducing the risk of online attacks.
- User control: Users have full control over their private keys and funds.
- Accessibility: Desktop wallets allow users to access their funds even without an internet connection.

Disadvantages:

- Vulnerability to malware: Desktop wallets can be vulnerable to malware or keyloggers if the computer is compromised.
- Risk of data loss: If the computer is damaged or experiences data loss, there is a risk of losing access to funds.

7.1.2.2 Mobile Wallets:

Mobile wallets are applications designed for smartphones and tablets. They offer convenience and accessibility, allowing users to manage their cryptocurrencies on the go. Mobile wallets can store private keys locally on the device or rely on a trusted third party to secure the keys. Examples of popular mobile wallets include Trust Wallet, Mycelium, and Coinomi.

Advantages:

- Portability: Mobile wallets allow users to manage their cryptocurrencies anytime and anywhere.
- User-friendly: Mobile wallets often have intuitive interfaces optimized for mobile devices.
- Multi-functionality: Some mobile wallets offer additional features such as integrated exchanges and dApps access.

Disadvantages:

- Security risks: Mobile devices can be susceptible to malware, hacking, or loss/theft.
- Reliance on the device: If the device is lost, damaged, or inaccessible, users may lose access to their funds.

7.1.3 Online Wallets:

Online wallets, also known as web wallets or cloud wallets, are web-based wallets that store private keys on remote servers managed by wallet providers. Users can access their cryptocurrencies through a web browser or a dedicated application. Online wallets offer convenience and easy accessibility but come with inherent security risks. Examples of online wallets include Coinbase Wallet, MyEtherWallet, and MetaMask.

Advantages:

- Accessibility: Online wallets can be accessed from any device with an internet connection.
- Easy setup: Online wallets often have a straightforward setup process.
- Additional features: Some online wallets provide integrated exchanges, staking options, or dApps access.

Disadvantages:

- Security vulnerabilities: Online wallets are more vulnerable to hacking attempts or phishing attacks.
- Third-party reliance: Users need to trust the wallet provider with the security of their funds.
- Limited control: Users do not have full control over their private keys, as they are stored by the wallet provider.

7.1.4 Paper Wallets:

Paper wallets involve printing or writing the private and public keys on a physical medium, such as paper. They offer offline storage and are considered one of the most secure ways to store cryptocurrencies. Paper wallets are generated using specialized tools or offline generators. Users can then keep the printed wallet in a safe location. However, it's essential to take precautions to protect paper wallets from physical damage or unauthorized access.

Advantages:

- High security: Paper wallets provide offline storage, reducing the risk of online attacks.
- No reliance on technology: Paper wallets are not susceptible to hardware or software failures.
- Cost-effective: Paper wallets can be generated without additional expenses.

Disadvantages:

- Vulnerable to physical damage: Paper wallets can be destroyed or damaged by fire, water, or mishandling.
- Inconvenient for frequent use: Importing funds from a paper wallet to conduct transactions requires additional steps and can be less convenient than other wallet types.

It's important to note that each type of wallet has its own advantages and considerations. The choice of wallet depends on factors such as security preferences, convenience, and the intended use of cryptocurrencies.

7.2 Best Practices for Securing Cryptocurrencies

Securing cryptocurrencies is of paramount importance to protect your investments from theft, loss, or unauthorized access. In this chapter, we will discuss best practices for securing cryptocurrencies and keeping your digital assets safe.

7.2.1 Use Strong and Unique Passwords:

- Create strong and unique passwords for all your cryptocurrency-related accounts, including wallets, exchanges, and online platforms. Avoid using common passwords or easily guessable phrases. Consider using a password manager to generate and store complex passwords securely.

7.2.2 Enable Two-Factor Authentication (2FA):

- Enable two-factor authentication on all your cryptocurrency accounts. 2FA adds an extra layer of security by requiring an additional verification step, such as a one-time password (OTP) generated by an authentication app or received via SMS. This helps prevent unauthorized access even if your password is compromised.

7.2.3 Backup Your Wallets:

- Regularly back up your wallet's private keys or recovery phrases in a secure and offline location. This ensures that you can restore access to your funds in case of device loss, damage, or theft. Consider using multiple backup locations, such as encrypted USB drives or hardware wallets, to minimize the risk of data loss.

7.2.4 Use Hardware Wallets for Long-term Storage:

- For long-term storage of significant amounts of cryptocurrencies, consider using hardware wallets. Hardware wallets provide offline storage and enhanced security features, protecting your private keys from online threats. Store your hardware wallet in a secure location, such as a safe or a lockbox, to prevent physical theft.

7.2.5 Keep Software Wallets and Applications Updated:

- Regularly update your software wallets and cryptocurrency-related applications to ensure you have the latest security patches and bug fixes. Developers often release updates to address vulnerabilities and improve the overall security of their software. Stay informed about updates and apply them promptly.

7.2.6 Be Cautious of Phishing Attempts:

- Be vigilant against phishing attempts aimed at stealing your cryptocurrency credentials. Exercise caution when clicking on links or opening email attachments, especially from unknown sources. Always double-check the website URLs to ensure you are visiting legitimate platforms. Avoid sharing sensitive information or private keys through unsecured channels.

7.2.7 Use Secure Networks and Devices:

- When accessing your cryptocurrency accounts or conducting transactions, use secure and trusted networks. Avoid using public Wi-Fi networks, as they can be vulnerable to interception and hacking. Ensure that your devices, such as computers and smartphones, are protected with up-to-date antivirus software and security patches.

7.2.8 Regularly Monitor Your Accounts:

- Keep a close eye on your cryptocurrency accounts and transactions. Regularly review your wallet balances, transaction history, and account activity. If you notice any suspicious activity or unauthorized access, take immediate action, such as changing passwords and reporting the incident to the appropriate authorities or platform support.

7.2.9 Educate Yourself and Stay Informed:

- Stay updated with the latest security practices and trends in the cryptocurrency industry. Educate yourself about common scams, security risks, and best practices. Follow reputable sources, participate in cryptocurrency communities, and engage in discussions to enhance your knowledge and awareness.

By implementing these best practices, you can significantly enhance the security of your cryptocurrencies and reduce the risk of unauthorized access or loss. Remember, securing your digital assets requires ongoing diligence and proactive measures to stay ahead of evolving threats in the dynamic cryptocurrency landscape.

7.3 Protecting Against Hacking and Phishing Attempts

Hacking and phishing attempts are prevalent in the digital world, and the cryptocurrency market is not immune to these threats. It's crucial to implement robust security measures to protect your cryptocurrencies from unauthorized access and phishing attacks. In this chapter, we will discuss strategies to safeguard your investments against hacking and phishing attempts.

7.3.1 Strengthen Passwords and Avoid Password Reuse:

- Create strong and unique passwords for all your cryptocurrency-related accounts. Include a combination of uppercase and lowercase letters, numbers, and special characters. Avoid using easily guessable information such as your name or birthdate. Additionally, avoid reusing passwords across multiple platforms to minimize the risk of a single compromised account leading to unauthorized access to others.

7.3.2 Be Cautious of Phishing Attempts:

- Phishing attempts involve tricking individuals into revealing sensitive information or login credentials through deceptive means. Be cautious of unsolicited emails, messages, or links that ask for your cryptocurrency account details. Avoid clicking on suspicious links and independently verify the authenticity of websites before entering any sensitive information.

7.3.3 Verify Website Authenticity:

- Before entering your cryptocurrency account details, ensure that you are on the legitimate website of the platform or service provider. Double-check the URL for any misspellings or variations that may indicate a phishing attempt. Consider bookmarking the official websites to ensure you access them directly instead of relying on search engine results.

7.3.4 Enable Two-Factor Authentication (2FA):

- Two-Factor Authentication adds an additional layer of security to your cryptocurrency accounts. Enable 2FA whenever possible, and opt for authentication methods such as time-based one-time passwords (TOTP) generated through authentication apps like Google Authenticator or Authy. 2FA provides an extra verification step, making it more difficult for hackers to gain unauthorized access.

7.3.5 Stay Updated with Security Measures:

- Keep yourself informed about the latest security measures and updates in the cryptocurrency industry. Follow reliable sources, read security advisories from wallet and exchange providers, and participate in cryptocurrency communities to stay abreast of current security practices. Implement any recommended security updates promptly to safeguard your accounts.

7.3.6 Be Wary of Public Wi-Fi Networks:

- Avoid using public Wi-Fi networks when accessing your cryptocurrency accounts or conducting transactions. Public networks can be insecure and susceptible to interception by hackers. If you must use public Wi-Fi, consider using a virtual private network (VPN) to encrypt your internet traffic and enhance your security.

7.3.7 Regularly Monitor Account Activity:

- Regularly review your cryptocurrency account activity and transaction history. Keep an eye out for any suspicious or unauthorized transactions. If you notice any unusual activity, promptly report it to the platform or exchange and take appropriate actions to secure your account.

7.3.8 Use Hardware Wallets for Offline Storage:

- Consider using hardware wallets for long-term storage of your cryptocurrencies. Hardware wallets provide an extra layer of security by storing your private keys offline, making them less susceptible to hacking attempts. Use reputable hardware wallet brands and follow the instructions provided to set up and use your hardware wallet securely.

7.3.9 Educate Yourself on Common Scams and Threats:

- Stay educated about common scams and threats in the cryptocurrency ecosystem. Be cautious of investment schemes promising unrealistic returns, fraudulent initial coin offerings (ICOs), or fake cryptocurrency exchanges. Develop a discerning eye for potential scams and rely on reputable sources for information and guidance.

By implementing these strategies and staying vigilant, you can significantly reduce the risk of hacking and phishing attempts on your cryptocurrency accounts. Remember, maintaining strong security practices is an ongoing effort, and it's essential to adapt and evolve as new threats emerge in the ever-changing landscape of cryptocurrencies.

Chapter 8: Taxation and Legal Considerations

8.1 Reporting Cryptocurrency Investments for Tax Purposes

Investing in cryptocurrencies comes with certain tax obligations that investors must fulfill. It's important to understand the tax regulations and reporting requirements related to cryptocurrency investments to ensure compliance with the law. In this chapter, we will explore the key aspects of reporting cryptocurrency investments for tax purposes.

8.1.1 Classification of Cryptocurrencies for Tax Purposes:

- The tax treatment of cryptocurrencies can vary depending on the jurisdiction. In general, cryptocurrencies are categorized as property or assets for tax purposes. Some jurisdictions may treat them as currencies, securities, or commodities. It's crucial to consult the tax laws and regulations specific to your country or region to determine the appropriate classification.

8.1.2 Taxable Events and Reporting Obligations:

- Taxable events occur when you realize a gain or loss on your cryptocurrency investments. Common taxable events include:

- Selling cryptocurrencies for fiat currency (e.g., converting Bitcoin to USD)
- Trading one cryptocurrency for another (e.g., exchanging Ethereum for Litecoin)
- Receiving cryptocurrency as payment for goods or services
- Mining or staking cryptocurrencies and earning rewards

- It's important to track and report these taxable events accurately according to the tax regulations in your jurisdiction. Maintain detailed records of transactions, including dates, amounts, and values at the time of the transaction.

8.1.3 Determining Capital Gains and Losses:

- Capital gains or losses are calculated by subtracting the cost basis (purchase price) of your cryptocurrencies from the proceeds of the sale or disposition. If you sell or exchange your cryptocurrencies at a higher value than the cost basis, it results in a capital gain. Conversely, if you sell or exchange them at a lower value, it leads to a capital loss.
- Different tax jurisdictions may have specific rules for calculating and reporting capital gains and losses. Some jurisdictions may require specific accounting methods, such as First-In-First-Out (FIFO) or Specific Identification, to determine the cost basis of cryptocurrencies. Familiarize yourself with the rules applicable to your jurisdiction.

8.1.4 Reporting Cryptocurrency Transactions:

- Depending on the tax regulations in your jurisdiction, you may be required to report your cryptocurrency transactions on your tax return. This typically includes providing information such as the date of the transaction, type of transaction, value at the time of the transaction, and any resulting gains or losses.
- Some jurisdictions may require additional forms or schedules specifically designed for reporting cryptocurrency transactions. Ensure that you are aware of the necessary forms and filing requirements in your jurisdiction and comply with

them accordingly.

8.1.5 Consult with a Tax Professional:

- Due to the complex and evolving nature of cryptocurrency taxation, it is advisable to consult with a qualified tax professional who has expertise in cryptocurrency taxation. They can provide guidance tailored to your specific circumstances, help you navigate the tax regulations, and ensure accurate reporting of your cryptocurrency investments.

8.1.6 Stay Updated with Tax Regulations:

- Tax regulations related to cryptocurrencies are subject to change as governments adapt to the growing cryptocurrency market. Stay informed about updates and changes to tax laws and regulations in your jurisdiction. Follow official tax authorities' announcements, consult reputable sources, and seek professional advice to ensure compliance with the most recent requirements.

Remember, accurate reporting and compliance with tax regulations are crucial when investing in cryptocurrencies. Failing to meet your tax obligations can result in penalties, fines, or other legal consequences. It is essential to educate yourself, seek professional guidance, and maintain meticulous records to ensure proper reporting of your cryptocurrency investments.

8.2 Cryptocurrency Regulations in Different Countries

The regulatory landscape surrounding cryptocurrencies varies significantly from one country to another. Governments and regulatory bodies have been actively working to establish frameworks to address the unique challenges and opportunities presented by cryptocurrencies. In this chapter, we will explore the cryptocurrency regulations in different countries and their impact on investors and market participants.

8.2.1 United States:

- In the United States, the regulatory landscape for cryptocurrencies involves multiple agencies and regulatory bodies. The Securities and Exchange Commission (SEC) considers certain cryptocurrencies and initial coin offerings (ICOs) as securities, subjecting them to securities regulations. The Internal Revenue Service (IRS) treats cryptocurrencies as property for tax purposes, requiring individuals to report their cryptocurrency transactions and pay taxes accordingly. Additionally, the Financial Crimes Enforcement Network (FinCEN) regulates cryptocurrency exchanges and requires them to comply with anti-money laundering (AML) and know-your-customer (KYC) regulations.

8.2.2 European Union:

- In the European Union (EU), cryptocurrencies are subject to regulations at both the EU level and individual member state levels. The EU has implemented the Fifth Anti-Money Laundering Directive (5AMLD), which requires cryptocurrency exchanges and custodian wallet providers to comply with AML and KYC regulations. Member states have their own regulations regarding taxation and classification of cryptocurrencies, with some considering them as currencies, commodities, or assets for tax purposes.

8.2.3 China:

- China has taken a strict approach to cryptocurrencies. The government has imposed various bans and restrictions on cryptocurrency-related activities, including initial coin offerings (ICOs) and cryptocurrency exchanges. While owning and holding cryptocurrencies is legal in China, trading and using them as a medium of exchange face significant regulatory hurdles.

8.2.4 Japan:

- Japan has emerged as one of the most crypto-friendly countries, implementing regulations to foster the growth of the cryptocurrency market. The country recognizes cryptocurrencies as legal property and has a licensing framework for cryptocurrency exchanges. Japan's regulatory approach aims to protect investors while promoting innovation in the cryptocurrency industry.

8.2.5 South Korea:

- South Korea has established regulations to address the risks associated with cryptocurrencies. Cryptocurrency exchanges in South Korea are required to register with the Financial Services Commission (FSC) and comply with AML and KYC regulations. The government has also implemented measures to prevent money laundering and illegal activities involving cryptocurrencies.

8.2.6 Other Countries:

- Cryptocurrency regulations vary widely across other

countries as well. Some countries have embraced cryptocurrencies and blockchain technology, providing favorable regulatory environments to encourage innovation and investment. Others have implemented stricter regulations, imposing bans or restrictions on cryptocurrency-related activities. It is crucial for investors to understand the specific regulations in their country of residence or the countries in which they operate to ensure compliance.

8.2.7 Evolving Regulatory Landscape:

- It is important to note that cryptocurrency regulations are still evolving in many countries. Governments and regulatory bodies continue to assess and update their regulatory frameworks to keep pace with the rapidly changing cryptocurrency landscape. Investors should stay informed about regulatory developments and seek legal advice to ensure compliance with the latest regulations.

Understanding the regulatory environment in different countries is essential for cryptocurrency investors, as it influences the legal framework, market dynamics, and investor protection measures. It is advisable to closely monitor regulatory updates, engage with industry associations, and consult legal professionals with expertise in cryptocurrency regulations to navigate the complexities of the regulatory landscape effectively.

8.3 Legal Implications and Compliance Requirements

When investing in cryptocurrencies, it is essential to understand the legal implications and compliance requirements associated with this emerging asset class. Governments and regulatory bodies are continuously working to establish legal frameworks to address the unique challenges and risks posed by cryptocurrencies. In this chapter, we will delve into the legal implications and compliance requirements that investors need to consider.

8.3.1 Regulatory Compliance:

- Cryptocurrency investors must be aware of the regulatory landscape in their jurisdiction and comply with applicable laws and regulations. This includes understanding the regulatory agencies responsible for overseeing cryptocurrency activities and staying updated on any changes or updates to the regulations.

8.3.2 Know-Your-Customer (KYC) and Anti-Money Laundering (AML) Regulations:

- Many jurisdictions require cryptocurrency exchanges and other service providers to implement KYC and AML measures. This involves verifying the identity of customers and implementing processes to detect and prevent money laundering, terrorist financing, and other illicit activities. Investors should be prepared to provide identification documents and comply with these requirements when engaging with regulated exchanges and service providers.

8.3.3 Securities Regulations:

- In some cases, cryptocurrencies may be classified as securities, subjecting them to securities regulations. This can impact how cryptocurrencies are offered, traded, and marketed. Investors should be aware of the criteria used to determine whether a cryptocurrency falls under securities regulations in their jurisdiction.

8.3.4 Consumer Protection:

- Governments and regulatory bodies are increasingly focused on consumer protection in the cryptocurrency market. Investors should be aware of their rights as consumers, including the right to transparent and accurate information, protection against fraud and scams, and the ability to seek recourse in case of disputes.

8.3.5 Taxation Requirements:

- Cryptocurrency investments can have tax implications, and investors must comply with tax laws in their jurisdiction. This includes reporting capital gains and losses, keeping accurate records of transactions, and fulfilling tax obligations related to cryptocurrency transactions, such as income tax and capital gains tax.

8.3.6 Cross-Border Transactions:

- Cryptocurrencies operate in a global and decentralized manner, which can give rise to complex legal considerations for cross-border transactions. Investors should be aware of any legal restrictions or reporting requirements when conducting transactions across different jurisdictions.

8.3.7 Intellectual Property and Copyright Issues:

- As the cryptocurrency industry evolves, intellectual property and copyright issues may arise. Investors should be mindful of any potential infringement of intellectual property rights when participating in cryptocurrency projects or using blockchain-based technologies.

8.3.8 Legal Advice and Compliance:

- Given the evolving nature of cryptocurrency regulations, seeking legal advice from professionals with expertise in cryptocurrency law is highly recommended. They can provide guidance on legal implications, compliance requirements, and help investors navigate the complex legal landscape surrounding cryptocurrencies.

It is crucial for investors to stay informed about the legal implications and compliance requirements related to cryptocurrencies. Failing to comply with applicable laws and regulations can result in legal consequences, penalties, and reputational risks. By understanding the legal landscape, seeking professional advice, and staying updated on regulatory developments, investors can navigate the legal aspects of cryptocurrency investments more effectively.

Chapter 9: Future Trends and Challenges

9.1 Evolution of Cryptocurrencies and Blockchain Technology

Cryptocurrencies and blockchain technology have already made significant strides, but their evolution is far from over. In this chapter, we will explore the future trends and potential developments in the world of cryptocurrencies and blockchain technology.

9.1.1 Scalability Solutions:

- One of the main challenges faced by cryptocurrencies, such as Bitcoin and Ethereum, is scalability. As the user base grows and transaction volumes increase, scalability becomes crucial for maintaining efficiency and reducing transaction costs. Various solutions, including layer 2 protocols, sharding, and improved consensus algorithms, are being developed to address scalability challenges.

9.1.2 Interoperability and Cross-Chain Solutions:

- The blockchain ecosystem consists of numerous independent blockchains, each with its own set of functionalities and features. Interoperability solutions aim to enable seamless communication and data transfer between different blockchains. Cross-chain bridges and protocols are being developed to facilitate interoperability and unlock the potential for enhanced collaboration and connectivity between blockchain networks.

9.1.3 Central Bank Digital Currencies (CBDCs):

- Central banks worldwide are exploring the concept of issuing their own digital currencies, known as Central Bank Digital Currencies (CBDCs). CBDCs could offer a digital representation of fiat currencies, combining the benefits of cryptocurrencies, such as fast and secure transactions, with the stability and backing of traditional currencies. The development and adoption of CBDCs could reshape the financial landscape and have implications for the broader cryptocurrency market.

9.1.4 Decentralized Finance (DeFi):

- Decentralized Finance, or DeFi, has emerged as one of the most promising applications of blockchain technology. DeFi aims to recreate traditional financial services, such as lending, borrowing, and trading, in a decentralized and trustless manner. The growth of DeFi protocols and platforms has the potential to disrupt traditional financial systems by offering increased accessibility, transparency, and efficiency.

9.1.5 Enhanced Privacy and Security:

- Privacy and security are paramount in the cryptocurrency space. As the industry evolves, there is a growing focus on enhancing privacy features and security measures. Innovations in privacy-preserving technologies, such as zero-knowledge proofs and secure multi-party computation, are being explored to provide stronger privacy guarantees without compromising the transparency and integrity of the blockchain.

9.1.6 Regulatory Frameworks:

- Governments and regulatory bodies worldwide are working

towards establishing comprehensive regulatory frameworks for cryptocurrencies. The development of clear and balanced regulations can provide certainty and legitimacy to the cryptocurrency industry, fostering widespread adoption and investor confidence. Striking the right balance between innovation and consumer protection remains a key challenge for regulators.

9.1.7 Mainstream Adoption:

- As cryptocurrencies and blockchain technology mature, the industry is striving for mainstream adoption. Efforts are being made to improve user experience, enhance user interfaces, and develop user-friendly applications that make interacting with cryptocurrencies more accessible to the general public. Increased adoption by businesses, financial institutions, and individuals could drive further innovation and propel cryptocurrencies into the mainstream.

9.1.8 Environmental Sustainability:

- The environmental impact of cryptocurrencies, particularly those that rely on energy-intensive mining processes, is a growing concern. As awareness of sustainability issues increases, there is a push for greener alternatives and more energy-efficient consensus mechanisms. The development of environmentally friendly solutions is crucial for the long-term sustainability of cryptocurrencies.

The future of cryptocurrencies and blockchain technology holds immense potential for innovation and disruption across various industries. However, it also comes with challenges that need to be addressed. By staying informed about the latest trends, developments, and challenges, investors can adapt their strategies and position themselves to benefit from the evolving cryptocurrency landscape.

9.2 Potential Impact on Traditional Financial Systems

The emergence of cryptocurrencies and blockchain technology has the potential to significantly impact traditional financial systems. In this chapter, we will explore the potential implications of cryptocurrencies on traditional financial systems and the challenges they may present.

9.2.1 Disintermediation:

- Cryptocurrencies have the potential to disrupt traditional financial intermediaries, such as banks and payment processors. Through the use of blockchain technology, cryptocurrencies enable peer-to-peer transactions without the need for intermediaries. This disintermediation could result in reduced transaction costs, faster settlement times, and increased financial inclusion for individuals who are unbanked or underbanked.

9.2.2 Financial Inclusion:

- Cryptocurrencies can provide financial services to individuals who have limited access to traditional banking services. With a smartphone and internet connection, anyone can participate in the cryptocurrency market, enabling greater financial inclusion on a global scale. This has the potential to empower individuals in underserved regions and stimulate economic growth in emerging markets.

9.2.3 Remittances and Cross-Border Payments:

- Cross-border payments and remittances are often slow, costly, and subject to intermediaries. Cryptocurrencies offer the potential for faster, cheaper, and more efficient cross-border transactions. By eliminating the need for intermediaries and leveraging blockchain technology, cryptocurrencies can streamline the process of sending and receiving funds across borders, benefiting individuals and businesses alike.

9.2.4 Tokenization of Assets:

- Blockchain technology enables the tokenization of real-world assets, such as real estate, stocks, and commodities. This allows for fractional ownership, increased liquidity, and more efficient trading of assets. The tokenization of assets through cryptocurrencies has the potential to democratize access to investment opportunities and reshape traditional asset markets.

9.2.5 Regulatory Challenges:

- The integration of cryptocurrencies into traditional financial systems poses regulatory challenges for governments and regulatory bodies. The decentralized nature of cryptocurrencies, along with the potential for anonymity and illicit activities, raises concerns related to investor protection, market integrity, and compliance with anti-money laundering (AML) and know-your-customer (KYC) regulations. Developing appropriate regulatory frameworks that balance innovation and consumer protection remains a complex task.

9.2.6 Collaboration and Partnerships:

- Traditional financial institutions are increasingly exploring collaborations and partnerships with cryptocurrency and blockchain companies. This allows them to leverage the benefits of cryptocurrencies while maintaining their expertise in regulatory compliance and customer trust. Collaborations between traditional financial institutions and the cryptocurrency industry have the potential to drive innovation, improve financial services, and bridge the gap between traditional and decentralized finance.

9.2.7 Systemic Risks:

- The integration of cryptocurrencies into traditional financial systems introduces new systemic risks. Market volatility, potential liquidity issues, and the interconnectedness between cryptocurrencies and traditional financial markets may pose challenges in times of market stress. It is essential for regulators, market participants, and investors to understand and manage these risks effectively.

As cryptocurrencies continue to evolve and gain acceptance, their impact on traditional financial systems will become more pronounced. While challenges and regulatory considerations exist, the potential benefits of increased financial inclusion, faster cross-border transactions, and enhanced efficiency in asset markets cannot be ignored. By monitoring these trends and embracing innovation, traditional financial systems can adapt and thrive in the evolving landscape.

9.3 Scalability and Environmental Concerns

As cryptocurrencies continue to gain popularity and usage, scalability and environmental concerns have emerged as significant challenges.

In this chapter, we will explore the issues related to scalability and environmental impact and the potential solutions being pursued.

9.3.1 Scalability Challenges:

- The scalability of cryptocurrencies refers to their ability to handle a growing number of transactions efficiently. As the user base and transaction volume increase, scalability becomes crucial for maintaining fast and cost-effective transactions. Traditional blockchain architectures, such as Bitcoin and Ethereum, face scalability limitations due to their consensus mechanisms and block size constraints.

9.3.2 Layer 2 Solutions:

- Layer 2 solutions aim to address scalability challenges by processing transactions off-chain or on secondary layers, while still utilizing the underlying security of the main blockchain. These solutions, such as Lightning Network for Bitcoin and state channels for Ethereum, enable faster and cheaper transactions by reducing the burden on the main blockchain.

9.3.3 Sharding:

- Sharding is a technique that divides the blockchain into smaller partitions called shards, each capable of processing its own set of transactions. Sharding can significantly increase the transaction capacity of a blockchain network by parallelizing transaction processing across multiple shards.

9.3.4 Improved Consensus Algorithms:

- Consensus algorithms, such as Proof of Stake (PoS) and

Proof of Authority (PoA), offer alternative approaches to the energy-intensive Proof of Work (PoW) algorithm used by Bitcoin. These algorithms provide scalability benefits by reducing the computational requirements and energy consumption associated with transaction validation.

9.3.5 Environmental Concerns:

- The environmental impact of cryptocurrencies, particularly those that rely on PoW consensus, has raised concerns about energy consumption and carbon footprint. The mining process, which requires substantial computational power, consumes a significant amount of electricity. As cryptocurrencies gain wider adoption, the environmental impact of their operations becomes a critical consideration.

9.3.6 Energy-Efficient Alternatives:

- Efforts are underway to develop and adopt more energy-efficient consensus mechanisms, such as PoS and PoA. These alternatives require significantly less energy compared to PoW, making them more environmentally friendly. Additionally, renewable energy sources are being explored to power cryptocurrency mining operations, reducing their carbon footprint.

9.3.7 Sustainability Initiatives:

- Various sustainability initiatives and projects are emerging within the cryptocurrency industry. These initiatives aim to promote environmentally friendly practices, encourage responsible mining, and offset carbon emissions associated with cryptocurrency operations. Investors and industry participants are increasingly considering sustainability as an important criterion when selecting cryptocurrencies and supporting projects.

9.3.8 Industry Collaboration:

- Collaboration among industry stakeholders, including cryptocurrency developers, miners, and environmental organizations, is crucial in addressing scalability and environmental concerns. By working together, industry participants can develop and adopt sustainable practices, contribute to technological advancements, and find solutions that balance scalability with environmental responsibility.

It is essential for the cryptocurrency community to address scalability challenges and environmental concerns to ensure the long-term viability and sustainability of the technology. By embracing innovative solutions, optimizing energy consumption, and promoting responsible practices, the industry can minimize its environmental impact while facilitating the growth and adoption of cryptocurrencies.

Chapter 10: Conclusion

10.1 Summary of Key Points Discussed

In this book, we have explored the pros and cons of investing in cryptocurrencies, providing valuable insights for individuals considering entering the cryptocurrency market. Let's recap the key points discussed throughout the book:

Chapter 1: Introduction

- Defined cryptocurrencies as digital or virtual currencies that use cryptography for security.
- Provided an overview of the cryptocurrency market and its rapid growth.

Chapter 2: Understanding Cryptocurrencies

- Explored the history and evolution of cryptocurrencies.
- Discussed the significance of blockchain technology and its role in enabling secure and transparent transactions.

Chapter 3: Pros of Investing in Cryptocurrencies

- Highlighted the potential for high returns through historical price appreciation and success stories of early cryptocurrency investors.
- Explored the benefits of decentralization, financial freedom, peer-to-peer transactions, reduced intermediaries, and accessibility to unbanked populations.
- Discussed the advantages of diversification and portfolio growth by adding a non-correlated asset class to investment portfolios.

Chapter 4: Cons of Investing in Cryptocurrencies

- Addressed the volatility and market risks associated with cryptocurrencies, including price fluctuations and market instability.
- Explored the lack of regulations and potential market manipulation.
- Discussed the potential for fraud and security risks within the cryptocurrency ecosystem.

Chapter 5: Investment Strategies for Cryptocurrencies

- Compared long-term and short-term investment approaches.
- Discussed the concept of dollar-cost averaging as a strategy for mitigating market volatility.
- Explored the importance of fundamental analysis and researching projects before making investment decisions.

Chapter 6: Evaluating Cryptocurrency Projects

- Highlighted the significance of understanding whitepapers and project goals in assessing the viability of cryptocurrency projects.
- Discussed the importance of evaluating team expertise and credibility.
- Explored the analysis of market adoption and competition to gauge the potential success of cryptocurrency projects.

Chapter 7: Wallets and Security Measures

- Explored different types of cryptocurrency wallets, including hardware wallets, software wallets, and paper wallets.
- Discussed best practices for securing cryptocurrencies, such

as using strong passwords, enabling two-factor authentication, and keeping wallets updated and backed up.
- Addressed the importance of protecting against hacking and phishing attempts through cautious online behavior and verifying the authenticity of sources.

Chapter 8: Taxation and Legal Considerations

- Provided guidance on reporting cryptocurrency investments for tax purposes.
- Discussed cryptocurrency regulations in different countries and the potential impact on investors.
- Addressed the legal implications and compliance requirements associated with investing in cryptocurrencies.

Chapter 9: Future Trends and Challenges

- Explored the evolution of cryptocurrencies and blockchain technology, including scalability solutions and interoperability.
- Discussed the potential impact on traditional financial systems, regulatory challenges, and collaboration between cryptocurrency and traditional financial institutions.
- Addressed scalability and environmental concerns, along with potential solutions and sustainability initiatives.

In this concluding chapter, we have summarized the key points discussed throughout the book, covering the definition and overview of cryptocurrencies, the pros and cons of investing, investment strategies, evaluating projects, wallet security, taxation, legal considerations, and future trends and challenges.

It is important to note that investing in cryptocurrencies carries inherent risks, and individuals should conduct thorough research, seek professional advice, and carefully consider their risk tolerance before making any investment decisions.

By staying informed, understanding the market dynamics, and adopting best practices, individuals can navigate the cryptocurrency landscape more effectively and make informed investment choices.

Remember, the cryptocurrency market is dynamic and ever-evolving, and it requires continuous learning and adaptability. Stay curious, stay informed, and approach cryptocurrency investing with a cautious and informed mindset.

Happy investing!

Don't miss out!

Visit the website below and you can sign up to receive emails whenever Alex Thompson publishes a new book. There's no charge and no obligation.

https://books2read.com/r/B-A-FEPY-MNHLC

BOOKS 2 READ

Connecting independent readers to independent writers.

Also by Alex Thompson

Alex on Finance

Financial Freedom Roadmap - Achieving Early Retirement through the FIRE Movement

The Art of Strategic Innovation

Standalone

Side Hustle Success: Unlocking Your Entrepreneurial Potential

Side Hustle Success: The Ultimate Guide to Passive and Financial Freedom

Mastering the Markets: Advanced Trading Strategies for Success and Ethical Trading Practices

Financial Fortitude

www.ingramcontent.com/pod-product-compliance
Lightning Source LLC
LaVergne TN
LVHW090418210926
848480LV00002B/611